# LEGAL BASICS FOR AUTHORS

ALICIA I. DEARN, ESQ.

Acid Squirrel Media

ACID SQUIRREL MEDIA LLC

Published by Fitz & Ferd Ltd. dba Acid Squirrel Media LLC. The names "Fitz & Ferd" and "Acid Squirrel Media" and their logos are trademarks of Acid Squirrel Media LLC.

Print ISBN: 978-1-965282-08-3

Ebook ISBN: 978-1-965282-07-6



https://aliciadearn.com

https://noaijustexperience.com

https://acidsquirrelmedia.com

# DISCLAIMER

This book is for general educational purposes only. It does not constitute legal advice and does not create an attorney-client relationship. The information in this book reflects the general law of the United States of America. The laws of other jurisdictions may vary.

Laws are specific to local jurisdictions, change over time, and may have changed since this book was written. The information in this book reflects the law as generally understood as of June 2026. No warranty is made regarding the accuracy, completeness, or currency of the information.

This book is not a substitute for the advice of a licensed attorney. Every legal situation is different, and readers should consult a qualified lawyer regarding their specific circumstances before taking any legal action. The author and publisher shall not be liable for any loss, damage, or other consequence arising from the use of or reliance on the information in this book.

# CONTENTS

# INTRODUCTION

I'm both a lawyer and an author. I was, in fact, an author first. I've been earning a living as a writer since 1998—when I got my first job as a technical writer while in college—and law is a writing-intensive job. Fair warning: I will use em-dashes in this book because AI learned off professionals like me, not the other way around.

I've also owned several businesses. I opened my first corporation in 2007. I've also legally advised businesses, large and small, since 2005. So I have a third skill on top of writing and law: entrepreneurship. When it comes to business, I've either advised on it or experienced it myself. And that is true, too, of my publishing business.

Most writers are creatives first and business people second. Many don't consider the business and legal aspects of creative writing until long after they've embarked on their career as a professional writer. But once you pursue writing for money (particularly when it's outside of a regularly held job), you become the owner of a writing business, the holder of intellectual property, a party to contracts, and a person who can be sued or who may need to sue.

None of this means you should shy away from being an author

because you can't afford a lawyer. It also doesn't mean you need to go to law school. Small and micro businesses get along without in-house counsel every day. But it does mean you need to know a few things, and that's why I wrote this book.

## Every Type of Author Career Requires Some Basic Legal Knowledge

If you've assumed that the type of author you are is the type who doesn't have to care about boring things like business and intellectual property law, you're wrong. If you publish books traditionally, your single most important business act is signing a contract written by the publisher's lawyers to protect the publisher's interests. That contract decides which rights you keep and which you surrender, sometimes forever. And after you get through that process, you still have to consider the content of your book, how you market, and how you get paid—all topics this book covers.

If you self-publish or freelance, you are not too small to avoid legal compliance issues. You must understand publishing and copyrights, how to make sales and take payments, how to hire editors and designers, and must know about what taxes and accounting responsibilities you have. If you use a hybrid or paid publishing service, you must still navigate all the headaches of owning a business, plus understand and negotiate the publishing contract. Even if you freelance (e.g. journalist or copywriter) or ghostwrite, all of these same issues will come up.

Whatever publishing route you take, legal tripwires are going to appear in your path. Mostly, they will be administrative headaches rather than lawsuits and audits (although those are possible). But you will have questions—and author groups on social media is not the place to find answers.

## The Author's Business Landscape

First order of business: start conceiving of yourself as a business owner, as well as an author. Every small (or micro) business owner wears a stunning number of hats, from accountant to sales to web designer to product shipper. And each of these roles touches on different areas of law.

You are a creator, which means you own intellectual property in the form of copyrights and possibly trademarks, and you must understand both how to protect your own work and how to avoid infringing the work of others. You are an entrepreneur, and you need to consider how to structure your business as an entity, how to keep its books, and how to keep its liabilities away from your personal life. You are a taxpayer, with obligations that arrive at least quarterly and in more varieties than you might expect. You are a party to contracts with editors, cover designers, narrators, assistants, agents, publishers, and distributors, and perhaps the legal employer of labor. You are a service provider or a retailer (or both) who sells directly to customers and therefore must understand payment processing, consumer protection and advertising laws, refunds, and chargebacks. And you likely operate on third-party platforms, from Amazon to WordPress to Meta, each governed by dense terms of service that define what you can and cannot do, in incomprehensible language, on pain of royalties or followers.

This is a lot of information for you to absorb, but you need not absorb it all at once. This book is your roadmap. The business you form in the first chapters is the same business that signs your contracts, owns your copyrights, and stands between you and a lawsuit. Work through issues as you build.

## The Real World Costs of Legal Mistakes

As I said, I have owned many businesses—several of which failed. I have also defended close to a thousand lawsuits. I've seen the ugly side of business mistakes. You won't be able to avoid making a mistake or two—I didn't and I'm a freaking lawyer—but this book should help you make fewer.

There are some pretty big mistakes that you do want to avoid, however. Don't sign away rights you do not understand you're granting to publishers and then watch helplessly as your work is exploited in ways you never intended. Don't operate as though you and your business are one and the same, because that's both more costly for taxes and opens you up to personal liabilities. Don't forget to keep your accounting records and end up overpaying taxes or facing penalties. Don't build your direct sales on a payment processor without understanding holds and reserves, and suffer from your launch revenue being frozen at the worst possible moment. Don't carelessly write about a family member or a celebrity and get slapped with a defamation lawsuit.

Besides these major pitfalls, there are a lot of scams targeting authors, from fake publishing offers to predatory marketing packages. You will come across them daily. Nothing angers me quite as much as companies who take advantage of a person's soul-deep dream to publish their artistic work by promising them results they can't achieve—or simply stealing their money. (I've got some stories to tell you in future chapters that may get a bit ranty.)

Knowledge costs nothing (okay, it costs the price of this book), and can help you build habits that make running your author business smooth and profitable. That's the reason this book exists. A few hours spent understanding the rules in advance is the cheapest insurance you will ever buy, and far less painful than learning the same lessons in a lawyer's office after-the-fact.

## Who This Book Is For?

This book is for the professional author who writes for money or a public readership. If you sell your books or articles, license your rights, hire help, market your work anywhere, post your stories or articles online, or intend to do any of those things, this book is for you.

It is written first for independent, self-published, and freelance authors, who carry the heaviest legal load because they are the publisher as well as the writer. It is nonetheless useful for traditionally published authors who still operate as a business, just with more outsourced pieces. Aspiring authors will find it valuable too, because the best time to build good legal habits is when you start your author business. For every author of every stripe, the second best time is as soon as you can, before there are any problems.

A note on scope: this book is based on the general legal principles of the United States, because that is where I practice and publish. While I have international readers, I cannot educate you on the laws of other countries. The specific laws of every other country are far beyond what one professional can competently cover. Where international laws commonly come up for American author businesses, I flag them as points for further investigation.

## How This Book Is Structured

The book is organized into parts that move from the foundation outward, roughly in the order a growing author business encounters each set of problems. You can read it straight through to build a complete picture, or treat it as a reference and jump to the chapter you need. The chapters cross-reference one another so that related topics stay connected.

Part I, *Your Business Is Not You*, builds the foundation: forming the right business structure; keeping clean books; understanding the taxes you owe; and handling the people you hire. These are the fundamentals that any entrepreneur must know, regardless of how they operate within commerce.

Part II, *Retail Business Foundations*, turns to the daily realities of selling: writing effective contracts; complying with the consumer and internet laws that govern your websites and marketing; protecting yourself from torts and liability; recognizing the scammers who target authors; and managing customer service, refunds, and reviews.

Part III, *Intellectual Property Foundations*, addresses your most valuable asset: your copyright. It explains how copyright works generally and how artificial intelligence affects it, the limits of fair use and the rules for using others' work, and gives you practical advice on fighting piracy. It also explains trademarks and how to protect your author brand. The final chapter is a primer on publishing and distribution rights, syndication, and consignment agreements.

Throughout, you will find plain-English explanations rather than legalese (as much as I can—some terms of art will sneak in—but I try not to let my evil lawyer side run the show entirely), practical action steps you can take at any time, and links to a resource appendix you can download for free. My goal is not to turn you into a lawyer, which requires far more training than this book could teach you. Nor is it to make you my client; I've semi-retired from law to focus on my own author business. Rather, it is to make you an informed and careful business owner who knows what to watch for and when to ask for help (from real lawyers, not strangers on the internet or a chatbot).

## Beyond the Basics

My first several drafts of this book included resources on topics such as FAQs about Amazon's Terms and dealing with account terminations, recommended software, and how to deal with disputes from demand letters to small claims. While I still think this information is helpful, it dragged the book down with too much detail because not every author will need it. The editor in me won out, and I cut it. This information now lives in an appendix that you can download for free as a PDF. Just use the link at the end of the book to claim it.

My author business is the most joyful business I have ever had. I wish every one of you outstanding success, even in the face of a mountain of AI-generated books. The words we write, the information we share, and the stories we tell are crucial to humankind.

***Keep reading and writing! And don't let the AI grind you down.***

# PART 1

## YOUR BUSINESS IS NOT YOU

ACID SQUIRREL MEDIA LLC

Chapter One

# BUSINESS FORMATION ESSENTIALS

When I was in college, I was a military spouse. I had two ideas for my future career: lawyer and romance writer. My (starter) husband made fun of the romance writer idea, so I went to law school instead. Which was fine; I also enjoyed being a lawyer for a while.

It was twenty years before I got the idea to write fiction again. And then it hit me like a fever: I wrote my first novel, *Conduct Unbecoming a Judge,* in three weeks, and it was a bit too smutty and had some amateurish mistakes. After that, I re-wrote it and wrote two more novels. And then thought, *I should publish these. How hard could that be?*

Hard, it turns out. But I blithely hired an editor, a cover designer, and a consultant to show me how Amazon's Kindle Direct Publishing (KDP) works. My first book was uploaded, and that's how I started my author business. As of the writing of this book, I've been at it for three years, and my (forever) husband likes me as an author far more than as a lawyer because I'm way less stressed.

While I haven't taken a scientific poll, I have a robust group of professional author friends who all started publishing in much the same way. You write a book because you have something to say or a story you can't stop thinking about. You publish it, a few people buy it, and somewhere along the way you realize you have to deal with the money side of it—hopefully because royalties landed in your bank account. You're also paying people, some of whom don't always deliver as promised. You're buying advertising and considering building a website. Or you sold a paperback out of the trunk of your car to a stranger at a local book and coffee shop. Congratulations! You're the owner of a small business.

So I'm going to tell you the same thing I tell every business owner I've ever advised, no matter what industry they are in: ***You are not your business. Your business is not you.***

What do I mean? I mean, you need to think of your business as a separate legal entity from you. You own your business. You work in your business. *But you are not your business.*

The law is willing to treat your author business as a separate legal person, with its own bank account, its own tax identity, and (in many cases) its own liability. But it will only do that if you set things up correctly and then respect the separation you created. Doing so is neither expensive nor complicated, and it can save you money long term, as well as prevent bad business deals from ruining your life.

### The Author as a Profit-Motive Business

When you sell your writing, you are putting a product into commerce. The format doesn't matter: you can write a Substack, sell books, freelance articles to magazines, or write product descriptions and emails for businesses. If you're selling your writing, you're in commerce.

Some authors worry about being classified as a "hobby" business by the IRS because it takes so long to build up a readership. What is a hobby business? If you run a business for years and years at a loss to create tax deductions, the IRS might consider it a fake business—something they may define as a hobby rather than a business.

This comes up a lot more in expensive endeavors, like breeding horses or racing yachts, but it could theoretically come up for authors. For example, if you're posting to your Substack for free and deducting expenses, you can only deduct those expenses for so long before the IRS thinks you're not trying to be in business, but rather just padding your deductions.

Some people worry about the Hobby Loss Rule, which can trigger scrutiny if you lose money in three out of five years. But that's not the whole story. There's no hard-and-fast rule on how many years you can lose money before the IRS gives you side-eye, and running a slow-developing business professionally can protect against any claims that your business isn't profitable enough. Follow the steps in this book and don't fear year three as a ticking time bomb for profitability. It's not that clear-cut. As always, if you have concerns about your particular situation, talk to your friendly neighborhood tax professional.

Most of us are trying to be profitable, and I am going to assume for the rest of this book that earning a living is at least part of why you are selling your writing. The rest of this book is based on the foundational goal of saving you money and avoiding liabilities so you can keep more of what you earn.

With that in mind, your first step should be to consider your business formation. That means intentionally choosing between being a sole-proprietorship, a limited liability company, or some other entity (corporation, benefit corporation, non-profit, partnership, joint venture, etc.)

### Sole Proprietorship vs. LLC vs. Other Structures

For the vast majority of you, the choice is between a sole-proprietorship and an LLC. The other types of entities are not useful for author businesses except in very specific cases. If you think you might need to be something other than a sole proprietorship or an LLC, seek legal advice (from a lawyer, not a paralegal or legal document company, and not an AI chatbot—their advice is frequently wrong!).

> >>> If you use a legal document company to help you create an LLC because you don't want to do it yourself or hire a lawyer, please don't accept their legal advice. I can think of at least two (who aren't included in my *Beyond the Basics* resources guide) who regularly give poor advice from unqualified individuals.
>
> For example, support representatives for these companies may not understand that an S-corp is a tax election, not an entity type. They may tell you to form your company in

Delaware, or they may tell you to form a multiple-entity structure. That advice is mostly built on urban legend and nonsense.

Once you start selling your writing, your default entity type is "sole proprietor." A sole-prop is an individual who runs a business without forming a separate entity or partnership. It costs nothing and requires no paperwork to begin. You simply report your author income and expenses on a Schedule C attached to your personal tax return. **For a brand-new writer with almost no income and almost no risk, sole proprietorship is a perfectly reasonable starting point.**

As you grow, however, the problem with a sole proprietorship becomes twofold: First, you are personally liable for your business debts and contracts—which is not the default in an LLC. If your author business owes a debt, you owe the debt. If your author business is sued, you are personally liable. Any time you are personally liable, your assets such as your personal bank accounts, your car, your wages, and even your home, are exposed to collection efforts. Second, a sole-proprietorship is more expensive from a business tax standpoint once you make more than nominal money from writing.

>>> If you publish with writing partners, things can get a little more complicated. Depending on the terms of your relationship, you may want to set up as a partnership, a multi-member LLC, or a joint venture (which can be between

LLCs or individuals). Business ventures with multiple people are outside the scope of this book, and if you're going to enter one, consider getting legal advice first. My resource guide provides a little more information on this topic.

Other than a sole-proprietorship, the LLC is the structure the vast majority of self-employed authors and small business owners choose because it provides meaningful protection and improves upon the sole proprietorship with very little ongoing complexity.

### Why Form an LLC?

An LLC is a separate legal entity that you create by filing paperwork with a state (usually the Secretary of State, but some states have different names for the appropriate agency). An LLC can own property, sign contracts, hold a bank account, and be sued, all in its own name rather than yours. There are the four main reasons to form an LLC: liability, taxes, privacy, and credibility.

**Liability**. An LLC creates a legal boundary so that business risks stay with the business. If a vendor sues over a contract dispute, the LLC is the defendant and the LLC's assets are what is at stake. Thus, when you operate properly through an LLC, a creditor or plaintiff cannot reach your personal assets without a separate theory of personal liability.

Understand, however, that while the liability shield is real, it is not a get-out-of-jail-free card. The shield protects you from the business's obligations. It does not protect you from your own conduct. If you personally commit a tort, e.g. you defame someone in your book or you punch someone at a book signing, you can be personally sued, because the law holds individuals responsible for what they do even if they are acting within a business.

The shield also does not cover debts you personally guarantee, which lenders routinely require from small businesses—so be on the lookout for guarantees in contracts. And it does not protect you from many tax obligations or from certain employment-related liabilities, where owners and responsible individuals can be held personally accountable. The LLC is best understood as protection against the contract and commercial risks of the business, paired with insurance and good practices to handle the rest.

**Taxes**. The reason an LLC saves you money in business taxes is because you can elect to be treated as an S corporation. An S-corp is not actually a type of entity at all, despite having the word "corporation" in its name. It is a voluntary tax treatment with the IRS that an LLC *or* a corporation can choose. A single-member LLC is automatically treated the same as a sole proprietorship for tax purposes until you elect the S-corp tax treatment with the IRS by filing Form 2553 (which can be found on the IRS's website for free—do not pay for it from online vendors).

The main advantage of an S-elected LLC is how you pay yourself. With a sole-prop, you pay self-employment tax on every penny of profit in a calendar year. Self-employment taxes include Social Security, Medicare, and Unemployment taxes. With an S-corp, you pay yourself a reasonable salary and take the rest of the profits as distributions—which are taxed like stocks and not payroll.

I'll illustrate: if your profit (income minus deductible expenses) in one year is $100,000, you would pay the fifteen percent self-employment tax on the full $100,000 as a sole proprietor or single-member LLC. But if you are an S-elected LLC, you can pay yourself a salary of $60,000 and a profit distribution of $40,000—and only the $60,000 will be subject to the fifteen percent payroll tax. You save $6000 in taxes on that $40,000 distribution. Once you're profitable enough, the savings are substantial.

You are also able to deduct some things with an S-corp that you can't with a sole proprietorship, with the most notable being a larger 401(k) allowance. This is discussed more in Chapter 4. But whether you're a sole proprietor or an LLC, most legitimate business expenses reduce your taxable income in the same way, and that is how you derive the net profit.

The secondary value of an LLC entity when it comes to deductions is organizational: a dedicated business structure with its own bank account makes it easier to track, substantiate, and defend deductions. Chapter 2 covers the mechanics of capturing them.

**Privacy**. An LLC gives you some shielding of your personal name and address. Some states (like Wyoming and New Mexico) allow for total privacy for LLC owners. Most don't. However, when you publish using an imprint (a publisher name, which can be the name of your LLC) and a pen name, that is what the public will see when they interact with your work, unless they go searching the Secretary of State for your corporate owners. For some writers who choose to use pseudonyms, this can be a major point in favor of creating an entity.

Besides your bylines and book covers, when you register your ISBNs, the entity listed as the publisher of record (your imprint) appears in industry databases and on the copyright page. Registering those ISBNs and your retailer accounts, including Amazon's Kindle Direct Publishing, under your LLC keeps your imprint consistent and professional and keeps your personal name out of the metadata. It also makes it cleaner to assign accounts and rights to the business as an asset.

You can use a DBA (doing business as) for your imprint for your ISBN if you do not have an LLC. Be aware that DBAs often have to be recorded with state or county resources so that people can look you up. Also, retailers and distributors will require your legal name instead of your DBA.

The unfortunate reality is that sometimes unhappy readers or customers will harass or doxx an author or business owner. The internet makes this easier to do at scale. While not perfect screens on their own, LLCs are an added layer of privacy protection.

**Credibility**. Operating as a named company rather than as yourself signals to the world that you're a serious professional. This matters more as you grow and enter into larger contracts. It also makes practical tasks easier. For example, an established business with its own tax identification number can open business bank accounts, apply for business credit cards, and qualify for vendor and software discounts that are not available to individuals. Over time, the entity can build its own credit profile, which keeps your business borrowing separate from your personal credit.

Contracts, invoices, and correspondence that come from a company rather than from a person land differently. When you negotiate with a distributor, audiobook producer, or license a subsidiary right, signing as the entity reinforces that you are operating a business and expect to be treated as one.

It is also easier to manage multiple pen names, projects, and branding through an LLC. Many authors write under more than one name, often in different genres. A single LLC can own multiple pen names and multiple imprints as brands beneath it, which lets you keep your finances unified while presenting distinct public identities to readers, and without confusing them with your legal name. The entity holds the assets of the pen name, so you can launch, retire, or rename a pen name without disrupting operations.

## The Optimal Timing to Form Your LLC

There is no universal right moment to form your LLC. But as a rule of thumb, consider forming your LLC when one or more of the following becomes true: you are generating enough income that the tax flexibility starts to matter; you are signing complex business contracts; or, you are selling directly to readers and customers. If you are about to release a book or product widely, set the entity up before the launch rather than after, because liability attaches to what you do, not to when you got around to the paperwork.

## Selecting Your State of Incorporation

Once you decide to form an LLC, you must choose a state in which to form it. The internet is full of advice urging you to incorporate in Delaware, Wyoming, or Nevada for various, vaguely explained reasons. For most authors, that advice creates complications you don't need. (That said, I admit I formed my publishing company in Wyoming, so the advice isn't always wrong.)

Delaware, Wyoming, and Nevada have genuine advantages for certain businesses. Delaware has a sophisticated court system that large companies and venture-backed startups value. Wyoming and Nevada boast low fees and strong privacy laws. While these features are real, they mostly will not be useful to a solo author who lives, works, and earns income in another state.

Your home state is almost always the correct state for formation. If you run your author business from your living room in Virginia, then for legal purposes you are doing business in Virginia, and Virginia will expect your business to be registered there. Failing to do so can get you audited by your home state.

Here is the trap that catches authors who organize their LLC in a state other than their home state: you also have to register in whatever state you are operating out of. So, for example, if you form your LLC in Wyoming but actually operate from Utah, you have not escaped filing in Utah. You have now created a Wyoming company that is doing business in Utah, which means you must *also* register it in Utah as a foreign company.

Now you are paying formation fees and annual reports in Wyoming, paying registration fees and annual reports in Utah, and maintaining a registered agent in both. You have doubled your paperwork and destroyed any benefits you get from being registered in Wyoming because Utah's privacy protections won't be the same. Forming in your home state means one filing, one set of fees, and one annual obligation to track. It keeps your structure simple and your costs predictable, which is exactly what a small creative business needs.

But didn't I just say my publishing company is registered in Wyoming? Yes, and not because I live in Cheyenne. I was able to form in Wyoming because I was not operating my headquarters in another state. When I formed my company, I lived on a boat in the Pacific Ocean. Then I moved into an RV and I traveled throughout the United States. I do not operate from one static place, and I sell online, so I was able to choose Wyoming as my company's residence. That made sense for me because, although Wyoming is actually not the easiest state to maintain an LLC in, it has privacy features I valued. But for the vast majority of authors, form where you live.

>>> A handful of states allow anonymous LLCs, meaning the owners' names are not required in the public formation documents or reports. New Mexico, Wyoming, Delaware, and Nevada currently offer this setup. An anonymous LLC can be a powerful privacy tool, but remember the foreign qualification trap: if you form an anonymous LLC out-of-state and then register it in your home state to operate there, your home state will disclose your information publicly. Some small businesses address this with a layered structure, such as an anonymous holding company owning an operating company. Those arrangements are complex and should be built by business lawyers.

>>> States differ widely in what they charge to form and maintain companies, which you should consider in deciding *whether* to form one, but not *where* to form one. For example, many states charge a "franchise tax" which is a special tax on business income and assets. For example, California has a minimum annual franchise tax of $800, which you have to pay even if you are losing money. So if you're a Californian, you may wish to stay a sole proprietor for longer. That tax cannot be escaped by filing in Nevada, despite what the internet will tell you, because you are required to also file in California as a

foreign company and pay their franchise tax.

**Registered Agents: What They Are and Why You Need One**

Every LLC must designate a registered agent in its state of formation, and in any other state where it registers to do business. A registered agent is a person or company with a physical street address in that state who agrees to receive official mail and legal documents on the company's behalf, most importantly tax notices and service of process, which is the formal delivery of a lawsuit. The agent must be available at that address during normal business hours. The state uses the registered agent as the reliable point of contact for the entity.

You are legally allowed to serve as your own registered agent in your home state, but it's usually a poor choice. Doing so puts your name and street address on the public record, no matter where you formed your LLC. It's the easiest information to find about a company, with data brokers syndicating the agent's name and address across the web. It also means a process server can show up at your home if you are ever served documents, which is an unpleasant experience that I wish upon no one.

Commercial registered agent services exist so you can run your author business in peace. For a modest annual fee, typically between $25 and $100 per year, a company dedicated to this work provides its address for public filings, accepts documents on your behalf, and forwards them to you. Professional registered agent companies also track your state filing deadlines and remind you when reports and fees are due (this varies widely by state). Missing these deadlines can cause a state to administratively dissolve your

LLC, and it's a pain in the butt to fix.

You cannot use a virtual office or a PO box for your process address for the LLC—it is legally prohibited in all states. Still, I recommend a virtual office address. It gives you an actual street address where mail is received, scanned, and forwarded. Because it is a street address rather than a post office box, it satisfies many services that reject PO boxes, including, importantly, most email services, banks, and merchant processors. It also looks more professional. Setting one up generally requires completing a postal form with a notary.

Most professional registered agents also offer virtual office addresses and mail services as an upgraded service, so you can use the same company for both. A traditional PO box is marginally cheaper, but it cannot be used where a physical street address is required, and you have to physically pick up the mail.

>>> Once you form an LLC, you will obtain an EIN (tax ID number) from the IRS and then prepare and sign a document called an Operating Agreement. Both will be required before you can open a business bank account. Operating Agreements have specific requirements for each state. My resource guide includes recommendations on how you can prepare one that is compliant with your state, and explains Operating Agreements with more detail.

**Action Steps: Forming Your LLC**

1. Decide whether you are ready. Triggers include earning

meaningful income, signing complex contracts, selling directly to readers, or publishing something controversial where you'd benefit from more privacy protections.

2. Choose your state, which for most authors is the state where you live and work.

3. Pick a name. It does not have to be the same as your pen name or imprint, but it can be.

4. Engage a commercial registered agent so that the agent's address, not yours, appears on public filings. Arrange for a virtual business address.

5. File your formation documents with the state and pay the fees. Note any deadlines for additional filings (for example, annual reports or statements of information).

6. Obtain an EIN (a tax identification number for the LLC) from the IRS for free, which you will need before opening business accounts. Chapter 2 covers this.

7. File your S-election form if you want. You can choose to do this when you form your LLC or in subsequent years at the start of the year.

8. Calendar your annual report and franchise tax deadlines so you never have to deal with a dissolved company.

9. Prepare your Operating Agreement.

CHAPTER TWO

# BANKING AND ACCOUNTING FUNDAMENTALS

I'll confess: I hate bookkeeping. I hate every single moment of it. I felt bored just writing about it in this chapter. Yet, bookkeeping is the number one trap entrepreneurs fall into when it comes to running a business, even if you're the only person in the business. I've lost count of how many problems I've seen in litigation, and even in my own businesses, when accounting got messed up or backed up. Procrastinating on your accounting today will make your life miserable tomorrow. Ask me how I know.

Proper accounting is not only how you stay out of trouble with the tax authorities; it is how you prove your deductions, protect your LLC's liability shield, satisfy your bank and payment processors, and actually understand whether your author business is making or losing money so you can make good decisions. None of this requires an accounting degree. It does require a system and regular effort to stay on top of it.

### Start With A Separate Bank Account

If you form an LLC, you are required to use a separate bank account. But even as a sole proprietorship, it's a good idea. Routing business money through a personal account is the fastest way to blur the line between you and your LLC, destroying liability protections (called co-mingling). And a dedicated account makes bookkeeping infinitely easier and signals to the tax authorities that you are running a genuine business (even if you aren't profitable). Open it in the entity's name as soon as the LLC is formed, and the EIN is in hand. Important: resist the temptation to pay a personal bill directly from your business account. Instead, pay yourself a transfer and spend personally from your personal account.

An Employer Identification Number, or EIN, is a tax identification number for your business, issued for free by the IRS, usually within minutes when you apply online. Despite the name, you don't need to have employees. The EIN functions for your business much like a Social Security number functions for you. Banks and payment processors ask for a taxpayer identification number because the law requires them to know who they are doing business with and to report certain income to the tax authorities.

An EIN is required for an LLC because it is a separate legal entity from you. You can also get one for a sole proprietorship and use it instead of your Social Security number for business transactions, which protects your personal number and reinforces the separateness of the business.

## Tracking Income and Expenses

Every dollar that comes into your author business and every dollar that goes out needs to be recorded. This is non-negotiable because you cannot file an accurate tax return and claim the deductions you are entitled to, or defend yourself in an audit, if you do not track your income and expenses carefully. Authors who skip this step overpay their taxes because they forget deductible expenses, or they underpay and face penalties later.

Recording income and expenses also protects your LLC because clean, complete books are part of proof that you are maintaining the company separate from yourself. They show that the business is real, that its money is its own, and that you are not simply using a company name to launder your personal finances.

Accurate bookkeeping is also crucial for making good decisions in your business. This isn't a business book, but suffice to say that cashflow is the single most determinative factor in your operations. It impacts everything from hiring to distribution and sales to marketing and advertising. You need to know how much money you're making, what you're spending, and what your business trajectory is. That's only possible through bookkeeping.

You will need a system. Your system can be modest, but it must be consistent. At a minimum, you need a way to capture three things: what you earned and from whom, what you spent and on what, and the documentation that backs up each entry (usually receipts and invoices). And this is why dedicated business accounts are so helpful. Your bank and card statements become an almost-complete record on their own, and then you can automate data entry into your bookkeeping software.

Decide right away whether you will track your books on a cash basis—which means recording income when you receive it and expenses when you pay them—or an accrual basis—recording them when they are earned or incurred. Ask your CPA if you need advice on this, but cash basis is almost always the correct answer for a small author business. It is far simpler and there's rarely a benefit to doing the harder thing. Whatever you choose, apply it consistently, because switching methods has tax consequences.

### Accounting Tools vs. Spreadsheets

A lot of people start with spreadsheets, so if you are one, you're in good company. Build a single sheet with columns for date, description, category, income, and expense for a simple ledger. Spreadsheets can carry a new author a long way, and it costs nothing. Its weakness is that it relies entirely on your discipline to enter every transaction and to categorize it correctly. There's no automation, and there's no way to reconcile using double books, which is what the IRS prefers.

I currently use a software called Wave. Wave is free bookkeeping software aimed at very small businesses. You can upload your bank and card transactions using .csv files, or you can pay an upgrade fee to sync with your bank and card accounts. When connected, it imports transactions automatically and learns to auto-categorize the expense type. It also produces basic reports and invoices, and has a rudimentary payroll module (although I prefer and use other payroll software). Wave, however, is my recommendation because, for micro authors, its low cost and extremely easy to use compared to other bookkeeping software.

I have also used QuickBooks and Xero for years in my other businesses. Quickbooks is industry standard for most accountants, and many are familiar with Xero, too. They are both more expensive than Wave, but they handle more complexity, integrate with several payroll services, and integrate with major tax software. If you expect to hand your books to a CPA for regular reconciliations and taxes, QuickBooks or Xero can make that partnership smoother.

There is no single right answer. Start with the simplest tool that you will actually use every week, and graduate to a more capable one when your volume or your tax situation outgrows it. The worst system is a shoebox of receipts and co-mingled expenses across personal accounts. The second worst is a sophisticated system you don't use.

### What Expenses Are Deductible?

So first of all, track everything you spend in the business accounts. But understand that some expenses are not considered deductible against your income—meaning that you will have to pay taxes on money spent on non-deductible income as though it was an owner payment. A good example of this is clothing. If you use your business account to buy clothing to wear to an event, you have to record it in the books. But when you categorize the expense, it will not be deductible because clothing is generally not deductible.

The tax code allows you to deduct expenses that are ordinary and necessary for your trade. Ordinary means common and accepted in your line of work, and necessary means helpful and appropriate for it. For authors, a wide range of costs qualify. Common deductible expenses include editing and proofreading, cover design and formatting, ISBNs and copyright registration fees, advertising and promotion, author copies of your own books, website hosting and domain fees, software and subscriptions used for the business, professional memberships, and the costs of attending writing conferences (including travel and lodging).

Two categories require special care because they are commonly misused and frequently audited. The cost of a home office may be deducted if you use a defined space regularly and exclusively for the business. That means that corner of your living room doubling as the kids' homework computer won't qualify. Meals and travel can be deductible but they require careful recording of mileage and meals are usually only partially deductible. The basic rule is that the expense must be for the business, and you must be able to prove it. A purchase that is partly personal and partly business must be split, and you should deduct only the business portion.

>>> Certain large expenses must be deducted over several years. Most author expenses are deducted in full in the year paid, but significant equipment or assets may need to be handled differently. When in doubt, ask a CPA.

### Income

Author income is more than royalties, and you must account for all of it. Failing to report income on your taxes can be charged as a felony and is a risk not worth taking. Authors can earn royalties, service fees, piece fees, licensing fees, commissions, and advances. They can also earn from direct sales.

**Royalties** are payments based on sales, whether from a traditional publisher or from a self-publishing retailer that pays you a percentage of each sale. Retailers and publishers typically report these payments to you and to the tax authorities, and they usually pay on a delay of a month or more after the sale.

**Advances** are sums a traditional publisher pays upfront against future royalties. An advance is taxable income when you receive it, even though it is technically a prepayment, and you generally earn no further royalties until the advance has been recouped from your sales.

**Direct sales** are payments from readers who buy from you directly, through your own website or in person. This income is entirely yours to track and report. Direct sales also raise sales tax and VAT issues, which are covered in Chapter 3.

**Other streams** multiply as your business grows. Examples include: subsidiary and licensing income from foreign, audio, or film rights; affiliate commissions; paid newsletter subscriptions; course or coaching fees; speaking honoraria; ghostwriting fees; consulting, editing, or service fees; piece fees for articles and short stories; and service fees for hourly or commissioned work. All of this is business income. Record each stream separately so you can see which parts of your business actually pay.

### Record-keeping Requirements and Audit Readiness

The tax authorities can examine your return, and if they do, the burden is on you to substantiate what you reported. That means keeping not just your bank and card statements but the underlying support: receipts and invoices for expenses, royalty and sales statements for income, mileage and travel logs, and the tax forms issued to you by retailers and processors.

Keep receipts, invoices, and bank statements for several years after closing that year's books. Most CPAs will tell you to keep supporting documentation for seven years. I keep my records for ten years because I'm paranoid, although I've never been audited by the IRS. Digital copies of records are fine and easier to organize than a shoebox, but if you don't have the time or mental endurance to scan all your receipts, keep them where they won't suffer from light, heat, water, pest, or pet damage.

### The Bookkeeping Habit

Bookkeeping is not something you should only do once a year for your income taxes. Build a monthly habit because it will save you hours of time, headaches, and heartache. You should upload your bank and card transactions into your software or spreadsheet at least monthly, if you do not have it automated. Delaying this will cause massive pain later; doing it monthly will take only an hour or two.

Review your books every quarter (and I recommend monthly) to catch miscategorized transactions while you still remember them, confirm your income from all sources, and make any required monthly or quarterly tax payments (for example, self-employment taxes must be estimated and paid quarterly—a subject further discussed in Chapter 3).

At least once per year (and I recommend quarterly), reconcile everything: match your records against every bank, card, processor, and retailer statement so that your books agree with reality before they become a tax return. A few hours each quarter prevents the pain of a year-end scramble. It also turns your accounting into a key management tool that tells you how your author business is doing, which helps you improve it, plan your growth, and optimize your taxes.

### When to Hire a Bookkeeper or CPA

A bookkeeper and a certified public accountant do different jobs, and knowing the difference helps you spend wisely. A bookkeeper handles the ongoing work of recording and categorizing transactions and reconciling your accounts, keeping your books current month to month. A CPA is a more expensive professional who advises on financial and tax planning, prepares and signs tax returns, and represents you in audits.

Many authors do their own bookkeeping and bring in a CPA once a year at tax time. Consider hiring a bookkeeper if you struggle to keep up with it at least quarterly. But beware, bookkeepers are a common source of friction and disappointment for business owners, so you will have to monitor to ensure you have found the right professional.

I hate bookkeeping, and so I have hired bookkeepers of all sorts for my businesses: from small accounting companies, to CPAs with in-house bookkeepers, to freelancers, to my own in-house accountant, to technology driven bookkeeping companies, to outsourced accountancy firms using overseas labor. I have literally tried them all and have spent hundreds of thousands of dollars on them.

Most ended in disappointment, to be frank. The best was my CPA with his in-house bookkeeper, but that was also the most expensive. And I hear anecdotally from my business clients that they also struggle to find good bookkeepers. That's not to say they don't exist; just that it might take you a few tries to find the right one for you. These days, I prefer to do it myself because my author business is not complex and I do not have a lot of expenses or any employees. But that's just me.

CPAs are a different story. I strongly recommend you get advice from a CPA whenever you have tax or cash flow questions, or are considering major transactions or new markets. You don't need to learn tax law the hard way when CPAs exist. (Note: a CPA isn't the same professional as a tax preparer at a company like TurboTax or H&R Block. Tax preparers are well-trained, but not nearly to the same level as a CPA, so keep that in mind when seeking advice.) Finally, the fees for bookkeepers, tax preparers, and CPAs are deductible business expenses, so when in doubt, use a professional.

### Banking, Payment Processing, and the Laws Behind Them

Running an author business means more than bookkeeping and writing. It means selling. And selling means moving money through banks and payment processors. Such financial service providers operate under a byzantine of laws that can cause friction if you are unaware of the basics. Understanding the rules just a little can explain why you are asked for so much documentation, why funds sometimes get held, and how to keep your accounts healthy.

### How "Know Your Customer" and Anti-Money-Laundering Rules Affect Authors

Banks and processors are legally obligated, under anti-money-laundering laws and what the industry calls Know Your Customer rules, to verify who their account holders are and to monitor for suspicious activity. These rules exist to fight fraud, money laundering, terrorism, and tax evasion. And they are not optional for the financial institution, which means, they are not optional for you.

This usually translates into requests for identification, your taxpayer number, business formation documents, and sometimes an explanation of what your business actually does and where its money comes from. None of this means you are suspected of anything. It is simply the institution meeting its own legal obligations, and cooperating promptly and accurately is the path of least resistance.

Authors who sell directly to readers, rather than only through Amazon, will typically have to answer more questions than you did when signing up for KDP. The same can be said for signing up for payments from a processor like Stripe, even if you are using it solely for invoiced services and piece rates, as opposed to a shop.

The reason is risk-related for the processor. And, unfortunately, a lot of this compliance stuff is run through AI and vast databases prone to data mismatches and opaque processes, making human verifications scarce when there are errors. When you sell directly, you are the merchant. That means you are the seller the payment processor is underwriting, and they don't trust you as much as they trust their huge data brokers, despite the propensity for data errors.

Processors (PayPal, Stripe, etc.) and banks also scrutinize new, low-history merchants closely, especially when sales arrive in bursts from a launch, when refund rates look high, or when the content is sensitive. Most processors will refuse to work with authors who sell certain types of content (for example, erotica, drug information including cannabis, and certain kinds of financial, legal, or medical advice).

Providing clear documentation about your business, maintaining steady and transparent activity, and describing your products accurately all help you clear these checks and keep your accounts in good standing. This matters because nothing is more blood pressure-raising than your sales funds getting frozen or your store being shut down without warning.

### Processor Holds and Reserves on Your Deposits

**Why processors hold or freeze funds.** When a customer purchases a product from you, they use a credit card or bank withdrawal to pay you. A bank withdrawal requires time for the money to clear the issuing bank—and, despite our many technological advances, they take several days to do this. Credit cards have to clear the processor and the credit card company (MasterCard, Visa, etc.), and they have to pass fraud and refund checks.

So when you get paid the funds after just a couple of days, payment processors such as Stripe, PayPal, and Square are advancing your money before they can be fully certain a sale will stick. If they fear future refunds or chargebacks, they protect themselves by holding back some (or all) of your sales deposits. A hold can disrupt an author counting on launch revenue, so it pays to understand the mechanics.

**Rolling reserves, fixed reserves, and account freezes.** A rolling reserve holds back a percentage of each day's sales and releases it after a set period, such as ninety days, so that funds are always cycling through. A fixed or minimum reserve holds a set amount as a cushion. An account freeze is the most severe: the processor suspends payouts entirely while it reviews the account, which can tie up funds for weeks. These types of reserves and holds do not happen all the time or to all sellers—in fact, they used to be more common than they are now, thanks to advances by Square, PayPal, and Stripe. But every processor has the right to do them without notice, so beware.

Common triggers for reserves and holds include a sudden spike in sales that breaks your normal pattern, a high rate of refunds or chargebacks, a brand-new account with no track record, large individual transactions, or a mismatch between what you said you sell and what the processor observes. The processor's algorithms flag the unusual patterns. Unusual is not the same as wrong, but it still prompts a review.

You can lower your risk by warming up a new account with steady activity before a big launch, by warning your processor in advance of an expected sales surge, by keeping refunds and disputes low, and by describing your products accurately. If funds are frozen, respond immediately and completely to every request for documentation, stay professional in your communications, and recognize that holds are usually temporary and tied to a specific concern you can address. If at all possible, have backup sources of funds to keep operations going during holds so you don't have a stroke dealing with customer service.

### Choosing Between a Payment Processor and a Merchant of Record

There are two fundamentally different ways to take money for direct sales, and the choice affects both your risk and your tax paperwork. With a payment processor, you are the merchant of record, which means you collect and remit sales tax and VAT; you absorb chargeback and hold risk; and you keep more of each sale.

With a Merchant of Record, the platform takes on the obligation to calculate, collect, and remit sales taxes and VAT around the world in exchange for a larger cut.

I chose Payhip for my direct sales because they act as a Merchant of Record. For a global author who dreads international tax compliance, a Merchant of Record can be worth the higher fee; for a domestic author who wants maximum margin and is comfortable handling tax, a processor may be better. This choice is explored further in the discussion of platforms and distribution later in the book.

## What Are Chargebacks?

I've mentioned chargebacks a few times now as risks when it comes to your processor. But what are they? A chargeback happens when a customer disputes a charge with their card issuer rather than asking you for a refund (or because you refused a refund). The bank pulls the funds back out of your account while it investigates, and the dispute is decided largely by the card networks' rules, not by you and the customer talking it out, and the outcomes can vary wildly.

When a cardholder contests a charge, their issuing bank initiates a reversal through the card network and requests evidence from your processor for the legitimacy of the charge. Your processor will then ask you for the information. You typically get a short window to respond with proof that the purchase was legitimate and delivered. The networks, not your processor, set the framework, and the burden is on you, the merchant, to document the sale.

Certain banks (American Express) are notoriously difficult on merchants and will almost always side with the consumer, contracts and delivery receipts notwithstanding. Others are notoriously difficult on the consumer (PayPal, CashApp). I have some thoughts on how consumer wealth disparity impacts the banks' rules on chargebacks, but they don't ask me. The fact is, this system isn't remotely fair to either small merchants or poor consumers—and it isn't likely to change.

That said, for most author businesses, it will be better practice to have a generous refund policy and to avoid chargebacks. Because chargebacks will cost you time, hassle, and banking relationships. Refusing refunds won't save you from the occasional scammer or pirate, either—there are better ways to handle thieves. The fact is, the more you sell, the more you will come across buyers who suck. You want to minimize their impact on your life and business.

Too many chargebacks can get you dropped from your processor. Card networks track the ratio of your chargebacks to your total transactions. Cross a threshold, often somewhere around one percent, and you can be placed in a costly monitoring program or have your account terminated. A merchant who loses processing can effectively lose the ability to sell direct, so protecting your ratio matters—and that's why I suggest refunding generously.

Worse, chargebacks usually carry a processing fee that you pay regardless of whether you ultimately win the dispute, and the original sale amount is reversed in the meantime. For less expensive items (like ebooks, which often sell for just a few dollars), the chargeback processing fee may be higher than the entire sale amount. A handful of disputes can take a chunk out of your profits, which is why prevention through clear billing descriptors, honest product descriptions, responsive customer service, and easy refunds is far cheaper than fighting disputes after the fact.

**Action Steps: Banking, Bookkeeping, and Getting Paid**

1. Open a dedicated business bank account for your business and route all business income and expenses through it. Never pay a personal bill directly from the business account. Pay yourself a transfer instead.

2. Choose your accounting method—cash basis for almost all of you—and pick your bookkeeping software.

3. Make sure you track all income streams to stay out of trouble with the IRS.

4. Keep receipts and invoices for every business expense. Digital copies are fine. Seven years is the retention period most CPAs recommend.

5. Build a monthly bookkeeping habit. Upload or sync your transactions, categorize them, and flag anything unclear while you still remember what it was.

6. Reconcile your books quarterly against bank statements, card statement, processor reports, and retailer royalty statements. Your bookkeeping should match reality before they become a tax return.

7. Consider hiring a CPA for tax questions, major decisions, and your annual return.

8. Before you set up direct sales, research your payment processor options and understand their content poli-

cies, documentation requirements, and hold practices. Choose between a payment processor (more margin, more compliance on you) and a Merchant of Record (lower margin, they handle sales tax and VAT).

9. If you expect a sales surge, give your processor advance notice. Warm up new accounts with steady activity before a spike. Have a backup cash source in case funds get held.

10. Keep your refund and chargeback rates low. Generous refunds are cheaper than chargebacks, both in fees and in the risk of losing your processing account entirely.

Chapter Three

# Understanding Different Kinds of Taxes

No part of running an author business (or any business) inspires more dread than taxes. Most of that comes from an overwhelming number of taxes that need to be paid, the massive consequences that you suffer when you get it wrong, and not knowing the full scope of what you're dealing with.

*I get it.* Taxes have tripped me up a time or ten.

Taxes are a dreadful burden on small and micro businesses. Far more than the expense, the burden is in the compliance and the mental load it creates. As a self-employed author, no employer is quietly withholding taxes from a paycheck on your behalf. That job is now yours—and employment taxes are not the only taxes that your author business generates.

You need to know what they all are. The goal of this chapter isn't to give you tax advice—I'm not qualified for that. The goal is to give you a list of tax types that may come up for your author business, so you can find the right tools, the right information, and the right professionals to manage them.

### Income Taxes and Estimated Payments

Your author profit is income, and the federal government taxes it—as do most states. If you operate as a sole proprietor or a single-owner LLC, you report your business income and expenses on a Schedule C attached to your personal return, and the net profit flows onto your Form 1040 along with any other income you have. You are taxed on profit, meaning income after deductible expenses, not on the gross amount your retailers paid you, which is one reason the bookkeeping habits in Chapter 2 matter so much.

The part that surprises new authors is that taxes are due as you earn, not in a single payment the following April. Because no employer is withholding for you, the system expects you to make estimated tax payments four times a year, typically in April, June, September, and January. These payments cover both your income tax and the self-employment tax described below. If you wait until your annual return to pay everything at once, you may owe an underpayment penalty on top of the tax itself.

The tax authorities offer a practical cushion known as a safe harbor. In general, if you pay in at least as much as your total tax from the prior year, with a higher percentage required for higher earners, you avoid the underpayment penalty even if you ultimately owe more, as long as you settle the balance by the filing deadline. A common and sane approach for authors is to set aside a fixed percentage of every payment that arrives, often somewhere between a quarter and a third depending on your bracket and state, park it in a separate savings account, and make the quarterly payments from that reserve. You will never feel the sting of a surprise bill because the money was never mixed in with your spending.

### Self-Employment and Payroll Taxes

Payroll taxes and self-employment taxes are birds of a feather. When you are self-employed, you pay taxes into Social Security and Medicare just like W-2 employees. Self-employment taxes refer to these contributions. For the self-employed person, they appear to be double what an employee pays because employees split their contributions to Medicare and Social Security with their employer. A self-employed person is considered both employer and employee and therefore owes both halves.

The combined rate for Social Security and Medicare taxes runs at roughly fifteen percent of your net earnings, with the Social Security portion applying up to an annual wage ceiling and the Medicare portion continuing above it. You may deduct half of this tax in computing your income tax, which softens the blow somewhat, but does not remove it.

Payroll taxes are a related but distinct concept that becomes relevant in two situations. If you hire employees, you must withhold and pay payroll taxes on their wages. And if your LLC elects to be taxed as an S corporation, you become an employee of your own business and must run payroll for yourself. This is where an S-corp tax election can save you money. Because you only pay payroll taxes on your reasonable salary—which doesn't have to be your total profit. The remaining profit can be paid as a distribution that escapes self-employment tax. But you should know payroll taxes also sometimes include state-imposed unemployment and disability insurance payments that you would not pay with self-employment taxes.

## State Income Taxes

On top of federal income tax, most states impose their own income tax on the profits you earn while living there. A handful of states levy no individual income tax at all, and some have rates that top 10% or more. You pay state income taxes in the place you earned the income, which is usually your state of residence. If you move around a lot, or take appearance or services fees for events outside your state, you'll need to get advice on how to handle state taxes from a CPA.

If you are self-employed, you typically make state estimated payments on a schedule similar to the federal one. If you are paying yourself using payroll, the income taxes will be deposited for you from paycheck withholdings.

> >>> Thousands of municipalities in the United States also levy income taxes and require deposits as frequently as monthly. This is most common in the Northeast and Midwest, and especially in Ohio and Pennsylvania.

## Business Licenses

When people start businesses, they sometimes think that they need a business license as permission to work—sort of the way you need a license to drive a car. Actually, unless you're creating commercial impacts in a residential zone, business licenses are less like a permit and more like a local tax. Some localities tax flat rates, and some tax based on the value of business property, all the way down to your office supplies—which is a real pain, so I hope your business isn't in one of them.

The rules on how much business licenses cost and whether your author business has to pay for one will depend entirely on the local laws. I couldn't possibly tell you what every locality requires, but I can tell you that work-from-home solo author businesses are sometimes exempt from business licensing and property tax requirements, so you should check with your city and county.

### Sales Taxes in the United States

Sales tax is conceptually different from income tax, and authors trip over it constantly. Income tax is a tax on your profit. Sales tax is a tax on the buyer that you, the seller, collect at the point of sale and then remit to the state. You are essentially an unpaid collection agent for the government, and your obligation to do this depends on a concept called nexus.

Nexus means a connection to a state strong enough that the state can require you to collect its sales tax. You always have nexus in your home state, where you physically operate. Other states may also impose sales taxes based on an economic nexus, meaning that once your sales in that state cross a dollar or transaction threshold, you must collect taxes on sales there even though you have no physical presence. The thresholds vary, but a frequently used figure is a hundred thousand dollars of sales or a couple hundred separate transactions into the state in a year.

A further complication is that states disagree about whether digital books are even taxable, and many tax physical and digital goods differently. The result is a genuinely complicated landscape for an author who sells widely and directly. One solution is selling through a major marketplace like Amazon. Retailers handle all the sales taxes themselves. But when you engage in direct sales, the burden falls on you to understand and collect sales taxes.

### Local Sales Tax Obligations

Sales tax is not only a state matter. Counties, cities, and special districts often add their own local sales tax on top of the state rate, so the true rate a buyer pays is a combined figure that changes from one address to the next within the same state. In certain home-rule jurisdictions, a local government even administers its tax separately from the state, which can mean an additional registration and filing. For a wide-selling author handling sales tax manually, this granularity is the strongest argument for using automated tax software or a Merchant of Record that calculates the correct combined rate for each buyer's location rather than trying to track thousands of local rates yourself.

And now you know why I said in Chapter 2 that I use a Merchant of Record. Using a MOR results in higher fees and more sales taxes being paid that you might exempt out of if you did it manually. But I just cannot be bothered with that level of hassle. I'd rather be writing!

>>> I cut a long and terribly boring explanation of things to consider when estimating whether you will have to pay sales taxes in your home state or states where you sell. For most

micro authors, you can avoid most sales taxes, and not using a MOR is a reasonable choice. I've moved this information to my Beyond the Basics resources guide if you want to take a deeper dive.

### International Sales Tax and VAT for Global Authors

The moment your books sell to readers abroad, you encounter a different species of consumption taxes, most prominently the value-added tax, or VAT, used across the European Union and the United Kingdom, and similar sales taxes elsewhere. Many countries require that VAT be charged on digital goods such as ebooks based on where the buyer is located, regardless of where the seller sits, and several have eliminated the small-value exemptions that once let low-priced items slip through. In principle, this can mean an obligation to register, collect, and remit tax in foreign jurisdictions, which is plainly impractical for an individual author to do country by country.

Two options make international sales manageable. First, when you sell through a marketplace such as Amazon, the marketplace generally takes on the responsibility of collecting and remitting these foreign taxes on the sales it processes. Second, for direct international sales, using a Merchant of Record shifts that entire global tax burden onto the platform. If you sell internationally and directly without either intermediary, get professional guidance—and godspeed.

### Franchise Tax and Corporate Tax Issues

As introduced in Chapter 1, some states levy a franchise tax or minimum business tax simply for the privilege of having an entity registered there, and you can owe it regardless of whether your business turned a profit. The amount ranges from a token annual fee to several hundred dollars, depending on the state. This is separate from corporate income tax, and is easy to forget because it is tied to the mere existence of your LLC. That said, many states waive the franchise taxes for small LLCs up to a certain revenue amount. So it's another area you'll need to check.

If your LLC has elected to be taxed as a C-corporation, additional corporate-level income tax filings are required. If you're thinking about going the C-corp route, get a CPA involved. When a business has enough revenue, it sometimes makes sense. But for most of us, the default pass-through treatment that comes with a sole proprietorship, a single-member LLC, or an S-elected LLC avoids a separate corporate income tax by passing the profit through to your personal return. (You'll still file a tax return for your LLC, but it is an informational return that gets matched against your personal return.)

### The Retailer's Role in Tax Handling and W-9 Forms

Because Amazon's Kindle Direct Publishing, and similar retailers, make up the bulk of revenue for so many authors, it is worth understanding what retailers do for you at tax time. (And these same principles apply to any retailers or distributors who pay you royalties, such as Google Play, Apple, or forums like Wattpad.)

>>> If you work for clients, they also report your income once they pay you at least $2000 (this went up in 2026).

Payment processors also report your income if you earn more than $20,000 or complete more than 200 transactions.

Before a retailer like Amazon pays you any royalties, it requires you to complete a tax interview, providing the information from a Form W-9. The W-9 simply gives the retailer your correct name and taxpayer identification number so it can report your earnings accurately. Retailers also verify your information for fraud and compliance reasons related to federal and international laws, which you may have noticed if you set up accounts with Amazon, Draft2Digital, Google Play, or the like.

At the end of the year, retailers report what they paid you on information tax returns and then send you forms documenting your royalties or other income—you'll recognize these forms as 1099s. Critically, receiving a 1099 does not mean your taxes are handled. The purpose of that form is to report income paid to you to the IRS. You also must report the income and pay the taxes on your own return. And you should know that the failure of your returns to match with 1099s logged to your tax identification and social security numbers is the fastest way to get a collection notice from the IRS (or worse, an audit or criminal prosecution).

Also, as the marketplace, Amazon collects and remits sales and VAT taxes on the sales it processes for your books. Amazon handles those because it is the merchant, not you. As a technical matter, Amazon is *licensing* your book and reselling it—that's why you get a royalty and not the full price minus transaction fees, like you would on Shopify. The royalty is a payment for the license you have granted Amazon to resell your book. Retailers who license and resell your books for a royalty are a hassle-free way to sell, but that convenience comes at a cost.

But the hassle of sales and VAT taxes is not a reason to avoid direct sales, which often carry the best margins and the closest relationship with your readers. There are plenty of good sales tax automation software that calculates, collects, and helps file the correct tax everywhere and that connects with popular shopping carts like Woo Commerce. You can also sell through a Merchant of Record like Payhip, who assumes the responsibility of calculating and remitting sales taxes and VAT in exchange for a small fee.

The through-line for every author, from the first sale to the best-seller list, is the same discipline introduced at the start of this chapter: understand which taxes apply to you, set aside money for them as income arrives rather than after, make your estimated payments on time, and bring in a qualified professional when the stakes or the complexity rise. Do that, and taxes become a predictable cost of a thriving business rather than the annual emergency or an expensive, penalty-filled trap.

### Action Steps: Planning Your Taxes

1. Learn about the different taxes that apply to your author business. Understand the difference between income taxes, payroll and self-employment taxes, business licenses and franchise taxes, and sales and VAT taxes.

2. Check whether your locality requires a business license and what it costs.

3. Open a dedicated tax savings account and start moving

money into it every time income arrives.

4. Set up your four federal estimated tax payment dates or your payroll deposit dates on your calendar right now, and develop a system for paying yourself.

5. Complete the tax interview and W-9 on every retailer and distributor platform before you publish.

6. When your 1099s arrive, check them against your income records and save them for your income tax filings.

7. If you sell directly to readers, figure out your sales tax situation before your first sale, not after. Start with your home state, where you always have nexus. Then decide: are you using a Merchant of Record who handles this for you, automated sales tax software, or a manual process? The same process applies to international direct sales.

Chapter Four

# EMPLOYEES, CONTRACTORS, AND YOU

No author builds their business entirely alone. At some point, you'll hire an editor, a cover designer, a proofreader, a virtual assistant, an audiobook narrator, a website developer, or someone to manage your advertising. Some of these hires will be straightforward contracting with professionals—like using a CPA or a lawyer who has their own professional practice. Some of them, like a virtual assistant, will be by-the-hour freelancers with open-ended scopes of work.

The instinct is to treat all labor as discrete service providers. You agree on a price, pay them, and move on. The problem is, just because you call someone you hire for services an independent contractor, that doesn't make it so—even if they also agree. Getting this wrong is one of the more expensive mistakes a small business can make. This chapter explains the rules so you can build your support team without inviting trouble.

### The Contractor/Employee Misclassification Trap

Every worker you pay is, in the eyes of the law, either an independent contractor or an employee, and the difference matters enormously. An independent contractor is a service provider who has their own business and multiple customers. I used the CPA and the lawyer as an example above because they are the strongest examples of professionals who provide services that are almost entirely labor, and often by the hour, but are properly considered your contractors and not your employees. You are their client, and probably one among many.

For an independent contractor, you pay them like another business while they provide services. You have no ongoing obligations and you do not pay their tax withholdings. Compare that to an employee. With an employee, you withhold income and payroll taxes, pay the employer's share of those taxes, carry workers' compensation and unemployment insurance, and comply with a plethora of labor and employment laws. That makes employees costly to hire.

Because employees cost so much more to engage, businesses are tempted to label everyone a contractor. That temptation is the misclassification trap. The label you choose does not control the answer; the actual nature of the working relationship does. If a government agency or a worker later determines that someone you called a contractor was really an employee, you can be liable for back taxes, the worker's unpaid share of payroll taxes, interest, penalties, unpaid overtime, and the cost of benefits you never provided.

Misclassification can cost you tens of thousands of dollars, so you don't want to screw it up. I'll give you an example. For many years, models for advertisements (let's say hair models for print ads) were paid like independent contractors. After all, they were only engaged for a single day's worth of work. Unfortunately for a bunch of companies, that turned out to be incorrect. I once defended a case where a well-known hair products company had a liability of $40,000 for a single day's misclassification of a model. That's an expensive mistake, and it wasn't defensible.

I also see this a lot with families who hire nannies, housekeepers, landscapers, and repairmen directly. Unless you're using an agency, or they have a business and you are one of many customers, your nanny or your housekeeper is your employee. And the cost of employee misclassification as independent contractors blows the minds of the people who do it unwittingly.

## Legal Tests for Independent Contractor Status

There is no single nationwide test. Different states apply different standards, and a worker can be a contractor in one state and an employee in another.

The common-law control test, used by the federal Department of Labor and the IRS, looks at how much control you have over the worker. It weighs behavioral control, meaning whether you direct how the work is done rather than just what result you want; financial control, meaning whether the worker has their own business, invests in their own tools, and can profit or lose; and the nature of the relationship, including written contracts, the permanency of the arrangement, and whether the work is a core part of your business. The more you control the details, the more the worker looks like an employee.

The so-called ABC test, adopted by several states for their own wage and employment laws, is stricter and presumes a worker is an employee unless you can prove all three of the following: (a) that the worker is free from your control in performing the work; (b) that the work is outside the usual course of your business; and (c) that the worker is independently established in that trade. Work is central to what you do, even if the worker clearly runs their own business—and that is where this test often fails.

For most authors hiring a freelance editor or designer who serves many clients, sets their own schedule, uses their own equipment, and is plainly running an independent business, contractor status is defensible under either test. The risk rises as you exert more control, make the relationship more permanent, or rely on someone for work that looks like the ongoing core of your operation. And where this is most likely to come up for an author: a virtual or marketing assistant.

### Common Misconceptions About Classification

Several beliefs lead authors astray, and each is false. The first is that a written contract calling someone a contractor settles the matter. It does not. The law does not care what you label the relationship; it cares about the substance of the relationship.

The second is that paying someone as a contractor, rather than running payroll, makes them one. The payment method follows the classification, not the other way around. Indeed, it is the collection of payroll taxes that interests a lot of state and taxing authority pursuits of misclassifications. The states especially have an incentive to pursue misclassification penalties and force more people onto payrolls because it increases their tax collections.

The third is that a worker who asked to be treated as a contractor cannot later be found to be an employee; the worker's preference does not override the law, and *the worker is not later prevented from filing a wage claim*. The fourth is that part-time or short-term work is automatically contractor work; a part-time worker can absolutely be an employee—as illustrated above, even a single day's engagement can be employment. Strip away these myths and you are left with the only question that matters, which is what the working relationship actually looks like in practice.

### Hiring Assistants

Authors increasingly hire help that sits close to the creative and personal core of the business, and these arrangements deserve extra care precisely because they involve more control. Someone who works set hours, takes detailed direction from you throughout the day, uses your accounts and equipment, and does whatever you assign, quickly resembles an employee under every form of misclassification test.

If you engage research help, a junior writer or ghostwriter, or a personal or marketing assistant, look honestly at your degree of control and the engagement's expected permanence before defaulting to contractor treatment. The more the person functions as an extension of you under your direction, the more likely they are an employee in the eyes of the law.

Virtual assistants and outsourced specialists, such as advertising managers or formatting services, are also usually structured as independent contractors. Sometimes that is appropriate because they serve many clients, control their own methods, and run their own businesses. Virtual assistants, however, tend to resemble employees more than a formatter you hired on Fiverr.

Two practical points are worth knowing. When you hire through an agency or platform that itself employs the worker, your relationship is with the agency, which carries the employment obligations, and you simply pay for a service. Sometimes this results in a co-employment situation, so make sure the agency has in its contract that they are responsible for all labor and employment laws and will indemnify its customers in the event of a suit.

Second, when you engage someone overseas, United States employment classification rules generally do not apply to someone working abroad, although you should still use a clear written agreement and keep records of payments. Also, and this is key, *the laws of their country apply*. So when you hire remotely, using a reputable agency that assumes responsibility for employment law compliance in the local jurisdiction is prudent.

## Government Enforcement and Penalties

Multiple authorities police misclassification, and they share information. This comes up most often when the IRS, the DOL, or a state agency suspects you of misclassification. They will share that suspicion with their federal or state labor and tax counterparts, and that's how one audit turns into three. I have handled this exact problem for many, many small businesses, and the danger is real. You can also get smacked with a fine for not carrying worker's compensation insurance as a cherry on top. When one agency suspects you misclassified someone, the consequences stack up fast.

My advice, learned from years of hard lessons as a business owner and a lawyer handling employment law cases, is not to hire too quickly. Use contractors for well-defined, limited-scope jobs where you are one of many customers. Hire your first employee when you're busting at the seams and your revenue can sustain the immediate cost for compliance setup.

If and when you grow enough to need regular help from an assistant, use a staffing company that is the employer-of-record or put them on payroll (with you! Since by now you should be an S-elected LLC). Modern tools make payroll and essential compliance manageable. Payroll software services calculate withholding, file the required payroll tax returns, handle year-end wage statements, and pay the various agencies on schedule, all for a modest fee.

While many employment laws do not kick in until you have five, six, or even fifteen employees, there are some that kick in the minute you have even a single, super part-time employee, and it's your niece. For example, you must register as an employer with the local taxing authorities and set up state accounts for unemployment and tax deposits, verify the worker's eligibility under the immigration laws (yes, even if it's your niece), report the new hire to the state, withhold and remit payroll taxes, and possibly carry workers' compensation coverage. Wage and hour laws governing minimum wage, overtime, pay timing, and recordkeeping apply, and you may need to provide certain notices and labor law posters to your employees.

Hiring your first employee is a meaningful legal event. Lean on payroll software or an employer-of-record service so compliance is handled correctly from day one. Hiring your first employee is also a good time to check in with an employment lawyer so they can give you the lowdown for your jurisdiction. They can give you recommendations on policies, handbooks, employee agreements on intellectual property (such as who owns art and written work product), and other details that you won't think of on your own.

Despite all the scary things I just said, building your team is exciting, and often the key to business growth. It doesn't have to be a roadblock for your business. Just go about it intentionally and carefully—don't add people to your team haphazardly because that's when things go wrong.

### Payrolling Yourself and The Bonus of a Solo 401(k)

There is one more worker to account for: you. How you pay yourself depends on how your business is taxed. If your single member LLC is taxed in the default way, you do not run payroll for yourself at all; you simply take money out of the business as an owner's draw, you are taxed on the profit regardless of whether you withdraw it, and you have to pay estimated self-employment taxes quarterly.

If, however, your LLC has elected S-corp treatment, you are required to pay yourself a reasonable salary through formal payroll, with the payroll taxes that entails, before taking the remaining profit as distributions. Paying yourself a reasonable salary in that situation is not optional; underpaying yourself to dodge payroll tax is a well-known red flag that draws scrutiny.

Paying yourself properly also unlocks one of the best advantages of self-employment: a solo 401(k). A solo 401(k) lets a self-employed author with no employees (or only your spouse as an employee) contribute both as the employee and as the employer, allowing far larger tax-advantaged contributions than an ordinary individual retirement account permits. At the time of writing in 2026, the annual cap on an employer 401(k) is $24,500 plus their match or profit share (which is typically small, e.g. three percent of salary, because it has to be the same for all employees). In contrast, a solo 401(k) caps at a whopping $72,000 because the employer profit share or match will be significantly higher.

Once you are earning six figures in sales, a solo 401(k) lets you shelter significant income from taxes while building financial security. This is especially useful for entrepreneurs who have had years of income instability and a lack of tax-advantaged fringe benefits while freelancing or building their business. For an author who has weathered lean years, the ability to catch up your retirement savings while enjoying the tax sheltering that brings is a massive win. It's one of the rewards that comes with succeeding in business after all the sacrifices.

Note: Once you hire employees, you lose eligibility for a solo 401(k) and the higher contribution limits. That is another reason I suggest starting with a staffing agency or PEO and "leasing" your first employee—keeping within certain rules, you can lease a part-time employee without having to shut down your solo 401(k). Most authors can and should keep their businesses tight, working solo or perhaps hiring only their spouse. Once you grow beyond that, a bunch of legal and financial consequences kick in; so step into that business phase with eyes wide open.

### Action Steps: Hiring Right and Paying Yourself Correctly

1. For well-defined, project-based work with clear deliverables, use a written contractor agreement with a scope of work, payment terms, and (if appropriate) IP assignment

clause.

2. If you hire through a staffing agency or platform, confirm in writing that the agency is the employer of record and responsible for all employment law compliance, including indemnifying you if a dispute arises.

3. When you hire your first actual employee, treat it as the legal event it is. Consider consulting a lawyer for a quick compliance check.

4. If you made an S-Corp election for your LLC, run payroll for yourself and pay yourself a reasonable salary.

5. If you're operating solo or with only a spouse as an employee, open a solo 401(k) as soon as your income can support meaningful contributions to enjoy a generous savings benefit and tax shelter.

6. The moment you hire a non-spouse employee, your solo 401(k) eligibility ends. If you're approaching that point, talk to your financial and legal advisors before you hire so you can structure the transition—including whether leasing through a staffing agency or PEO preserves your plan for a while longer.

# PART II

## RETAIL BUSINESS FOUNDATIONS

Acid Squirrel Media

ACID SQUIRREL MEDIA LLC

Chapter Five

# EFFECTIVE AGREEMENTS

A contract is a promise the law will enforce, and they don't have to be written down (but they should be). For an author, contracts are everywhere: the agreement with your editor, the deal with your cover designer, the terms of service with your retailers and payment processors. Most of the time, these relationships go smoothly and the contract is never consulted. The contract really earns its keep when something goes wrong. And that's when the difference between a clear written agreement and a vague verbal understanding is most stark. A good agreement is often the difference between a quick resolution to a disagreement and a ruinous dispute.

## Why Contracts Matter

I have yet to meet any business owner or self-employed person who hasn't had a contract dispute. When it comes to authorship, consider these familiar scenarios. An author pays a designer half up front for a cover, the designer disappears, and there is nothing in writing about deadlines or refunds. An author hires a line editor, the work that comes back is unusable, and the two of them have wildly different memories of what was promised. A ghostwriter delivers a manuscript and then claims to still own it because nothing assigned the rights (I once represented a client in this exact situation, which turned into an extremely ugly lawsuit—neither the company nor the writer had any experience in ghostwriting before and it was a mess). A narrator records an audiobook, the author later wants to distribute it somewhere the narrator objects to, and no one addressed rights.

In every one of these situations, a well-written agreement would have defined expectations in advance and given the wronged party a clear remedy. Without it, the parties are left arguing over what they each remember, which is an expensive and unreliable way to resolve anything.

Writing up a contract does three useful things at once. It forces both sides to think through and agree on the details before money changes hands, surfacing misunderstandings while they are still cheap to fix. It creates a record of what was agreed, so memory and good faith are not the only safeguards. And it gives you enforceable rights if the other side fails to perform. None of that requires the agreement to be long or intimidating. It requires it to be clear and, most importantly, to *exist*.

### Key Elements of a Solid Agreement

I can't teach you everything you need to know about writing contracts in 2000 words. To be completely frank, it takes a lawyer years of experience, both in negotiations and in litigation, to spot the cracks in contracts. That's not knowledge I could download into your head outside of The Matrix.

But you can get a long way using reliable templates, risk mitigation (i.e. use lawyers when a lot of money or rights is at stake, and DIY it when the stakes are less than the lawyers' hourly rate), and thoughtfulness. My resource guide gives some suggestions on how to source both templates and lawyers.

A well-written contract does not use archaic language, but it does need to cover some essentials. At minimum, a solid agreement identifies the parties by their full legal or business names, describes the work or deliverables in concrete detail, states the price and the payment terms, sets a timeline with dates, and specifies who owns the resulting intellectual property. From there, the agreements that protect you best also address confidentiality where sensitive material is involved, what happens if either party wants to end the arrangement (called termination), warranties or promises each side is making, and how disputes will be handled if they arise. Each of these elements answers a question that, left unanswered, becomes the seed of a later, expensive legal fight.

Templates are genuinely useful—when from a reputable source. For routine, low-risk arrangements they will usually suffice. The danger lies in where you get them and how blindly you use them. A contract template pulled from an anonymous corner of the internet may be outdated, may be written for the law of a different state or country, may favor the party who originally drafted it, or may simply be wrong. A template generated by a general artificial intelligence tool carries similar risks: it can read smoothly while omitting a crucial clause, misstating the law, or including provisions that do not fit your situation, and it cannot account for facts it was never told. Using such a document without understanding it can cause trouble down the road.

The safer sources are templates drafted by qualified attorneys, agreements provided through reputable professional and author organizations, and forms you have had reviewed or adapted by a lawyer for your jurisdiction. A modest investment in a sound template that you then reuse across many similar engagements spreads the cost across years of agreements—although I caution you against replicating contracts without thought as to the specifics of any particular deal, because that's how a once good contract goes bad.

And it goes without saying: However the contract comes into being, read every clause and make sure you understand and agree with it before you sign.

### Clarity over Legalese: Practical Drafting Tips

Contracts should not be dense with old-fashioned legal jargon, and that is often the sign of poor drafting or lazy lawyering. A contract does not typically require magic words from the eighteenth century. Rather, it is interpreted according to what its words mean today, and plain, specific language is both fully enforceable and far less likely to be misunderstood.

If you're going to write it yourself, write in direct sentences. You're not James Joyce, so don't write entire pages of stream-of-consciousness, or four thousand word clauses. Say what you mean, precisely as you mean it. Where a term could be read in two ways, clarify it. Replace vague promises with concrete specifics. Define terms that have special meanings beyond what the dictionary says. The aim is an agreement that both parties, neither of whom being lawyers, can read and understand it in the same way. Because a contract that is clear to its signers is a contract that rarely needs a judge to interpret it.

### Milestones, Deliverables, and Payment Terms

Money and work product are the heart of most contracts, and ambiguity here causes the most trouble. Describe the deliverable precisely: not merely an edit, but a developmental edit of a manuscript of a stated length, returned in a specified format, including a defined number of revision passes. Tie payments to milestones rather than leaving them open. A common structure pays a deposit to begin, one or more payments at defined checkpoints, and a final payment on acceptance of the completed work, with the standard for acceptance spelled out so it is not purely subjective. State the currency, the method, and the due dates. Address what happens if a deadline is missed by either side, and whether payments are refundable, and under what conditions. The clearer the link between specific work and specific payment, the less room there is for the disputes that arise when one side feels it gave more than it got.

### Enforcement Provisions and Dispute Resolution

A contract is only as good as your ability to enforce it, so think ahead about what happens if the other side breaches. A well-built agreement says how disputes will be resolved and where. It can specify which state's law governs the agreement and in which location any dispute will be heard, which matters enormously when you and a contractor are in different states or countries, because litigating far from home is costly and discouraging. It can require the parties to attempt informal resolution or mediation before escalating. Thinking through these mechanics while everyone is still friendly produces far better terms than trying to sort them out in the heat of a conflict.

### Arbitration and ADR vs. Litigation

Disputes can be resolved in court through litigation or outside court through alternative dispute resolution, which typically means mediation and/or arbitration. The distinctions matter because contracts often dictate which path you must take.

Litigation is the public court system. It offers strong procedural protections and the right to appeal, but it is typically slow, expensive, and a matter of public record. Small claims, however, can be a quick and inexpensive forum for resolving disputes that require a judge.

Mediation uses a neutral third party to help the sides negotiate a settlement. It is non-binding, confidential, relatively cheap and fast (compared to litigation, anyway), and it preserves relationships. But it only works if both sides will compromise.

Arbitration puts the decision in the hands of a private arbitrator who acts like a judge. The arbitrator's decision is usually binding with very limited appeal rights. It is generally faster and more private than court, but it can still be expensive. And binding arbitration means giving up your rights to a jury trial and to appeals.

For an author, a sensible contract often calls for mediation first, reserving the heavy machinery for disputes that cannot be resolved informally. Be cautious about agreeing to jurisdiction in a distant location, since that can make it impractical to pursue even a strong claim. Be also mindful of the costs of mediation and arbitration as compared to limited jurisdiction courts (like small claims). In the resources guide, I list some resources for cheap and effective ways to resolve disputes that you can build into your agreements.

### Attorneys' Fees Clauses

This single clause deserves its own attention because in litigation, attorneys' fees far too often drive the entire train. Under the default rule in the United States, each side in a dispute pays its own legal fees regardless of who wins. That rule has a harsh consequence for small matters: if a contractor owes you a few thousand dollars, the cost of hiring a lawyer to pursue it can exceed what you are owed, which is precisely why some parties feel free to breach contracts, betting you will not find it worth chasing them.

An attorneys' fees clause can change that calculation. A provision stating that the prevailing party in a dispute may recover its reasonable attorneys' fees from the losing party makes it economically feasible to enforce the agreement and discourages the other side from breaching in the first place, because they risk paying for both sides' lawyers. Make the clause mutual, so it applies to whomever prevails, both because that is fair and because one-sided fee clauses are sometimes disfavored or outright unenforceable, depending on the jurisdiction. For a small business, a well-drafted prevailing-party fee clause is one of the most valuable sentences a contract can contain.

### When to Hire a Lawyer vs. Using Templates

Not every agreement justifies a lawyer's involvement, and not every agreement is safe without one. The deciding factors are the stakes and the complexity. For routine, lower-value, standardized engagements, such as a basic agreement with an editor or designer, a sound template that you understand and adapt is usually sufficient.

For high-value, long-term, or employee agreements, for anything that transfers significant rights, for agreements you do not fully understand, or for contracts presented by the other side with the help of their own lawyer, the cost of hiring a lawyer to review is often worthwhile. You should use a lawyer for most publishing, distribution, licensing, and audiobook production agreements. The general principle is simple: match the level of protection to the level of risk, and never sign something you don't understand.

**Action Steps: Creating Effective Agreements**

1. Transactions should be in writing whenever feasible—especially ones with long-term performance or where a lot of money or property rights are at stake. Use an attorney when the stakes justify the expense.

2. When you use templates, source them from qualified attorneys or reputable author organizations. Don't use templates from random corners of the internet, and don't trust AI-generated contracts because you won't be able to tell whether they are correctly drafted.

3. When you write contracts, clear language and specificity is the rule. You don't need magic archaic legalese, and actually it is undesirable.

4. Good contracts include: the parties identified by their full legal or business names; the deliverable described in specific detail; the price and payment terms; a timeline for deliverables; and who owns the resulting intellectual

property.

5. An IP assignment clause is especially important in agreements with editors, designers, formatters, ghostwriters, narrators, and anyone else creating work product for your business.

6. Tie payments to milestones whenever possible. A common structure is a deposit to start, payments at defined checkpoints, and a final payment on acceptance of completed work.

7. Include dispute resolution clauses specifying which state's law governs, where disputes will be heard (jurisdiction and venue), and whether mediation or arbitration are required before escalating. Add a mutual prevailing-party attorneys' fees clause to your contracts.

Chapter Six

# CONSUMER LAWS AND WEB COMPLIANCE

So far in this book, we've been talking about all the ways we spend money to operate a business: incorporating, taxes, banking fees, accountants and bookkeeping, hiring help, contracts, etc. In order to afford all these things, you need to make money. And that second half of the equation carries its own legal risks, because now you're interfacing with the *public*.

Anything you do to sell your work, from developing a website, running an email list, buying and posting ads, and marketing or pitching your work to customers or readers, is regulated. The regulations aren't as extensive as the regulations surrounding taxes and employees, which is the good news. They still create some headaches, which is the bad news.

The rule of thumb is that you can't do things that are misleading or sneaky. Consumer laws are in place to prevent fraud and abuse of the buying public, and to prevent harm to children.

I know what you're thinking: *Great! I'm not shady, so I don't need to worry about this part.* Not so fast. There are some things you have to do to make sure you aren't mistaken for a pirate, scammer, or predatory. The good news is that, so long as you adhere to these standards, your risks of liability, lawsuits, and prosecution are pretty low.

Websites are a good place to start because most businesses have them—or at least online profiles. Even if you don't host your own website, the below laws will still apply to your online presence, however you have it. And some laws apply to offline commerce as well (e.g. advertising in print).

Websites have four major areas of compliance. First, your website can't lie to people. In other words, your advertising and copy must be honest and fair. The same goes for your privacy policies and terms of service. And your duty to present your words carefully is heightened if your audience includes children.

Second, if you collect information about people, you must disclose it and protect it. This is another place where privacy policies matter. This is also where cookie warnings are required in the EU. And, most seriously, there are laws that protect the collecting and storage of financial information as part of the sales process.

Third, commercial websites must be accessible. This is an area of increased targeting for lawsuits, so you should know what is required of you to comply. And fourth, you must own the rights to the content on your website, including images. That means your words are your own and the images are yours or licensed to you by the creator for commercial use. This is covered in detail in Chapter 10.

## Advertising and the FTC

When you promote your books using any kind of communication—be it words, videos, audio, or images—you are advertising. And, in a nutshell, advertising must not be deceptive. Obvious lies are easy to avoid. Where this comes up is usually more subtle.

I most recently came across this with a company that sold marketing services to authors. This agency had a "guarantee" on their sales page, and it heavily implied that the guarantee was a refund if the buyer was unhappy with their product. I purchased their first-tier product, which was not very expensive, so I took a chance because they offered a guarantee.

After purchase, I was not satisfied and went to their sales page to request a refund a few days later. That is when I noticed that their terms of service did not define their guarantee. And no part of their sales page specified the process for obtaining a refund. Nor was there any contact information. I started to be annoyed that I hadn't noticed this sooner because these are hallmarks of dishonest practices.

It was approximately $20 at stake, but I sometimes do things on principle. So with the help of Google and Instagram, I was able to locate their general business page (it was a different URL from their sales page) and a contact form. I emailed them and requested the refund.

The next day, I got a response that said they don't give refunds. Rather, their "guarantee" was customer support to address my concerns so that I could find their product useful. Interesting, since the sales page had no customer support information, nor did it specify that this was the guarantee's substance.

This was unacceptable, so I sent them an extensive response

citing all the consumer laws they were breaking and suggested that it would be far cheaper to refund me than to make me mad. I suggested they also use a lawyer to get their sales pages into compliance. To their credit, they refunded me and fixed their advertising and terms of service, although their (clearly lawyer-drafted) responsive email was a tad snippy.

The Federal Trade Commission enforces over eighty laws aimed at preventing deceptive trade. Most states also have consumer laws, sometimes referred to as mini-FTC acts. Not all of these laws carry the risk of private lawsuits, but they all carry the risk of prosecution by the FTC or state attorneys general.

The upshot is: say what you mean and mean what you say; don't exaggerate; don't lie by omission; don't imply celebrity endorsements or fake reviews; and don't make medical, legal, or financial promises that you are not qualified to make.

The same honesty principle applies to scarcity and urgency tactics. A "limited time only" offer or a countdown timer should be real, not a manufactured trick that resets every time someone visits the page. Customers notice such things, and your practices will impact your reputation and, eventually, your sales.

>>> AI-generated content should be disclosed. The FTC has been increasingly aggressive about disclosure and authenticity requirements in the digital commerce space. Consumers and marketplaces are also very aggressive about this. One of the fastest ways currently to crash an author's career is to use AI and not disclose it.

>>> When it comes to reviews and testimonials, it is legitimate to ask readers to leave an honest review and direct them to sites. What violates the terms of service of the major platforms is paying for reviews or encouraging fake reviews (e.g. from friends or farms). Incentivized reviews, where a benefit is tied to leaving a review, are prohibited by major retailers and can also run afoul of truth-in-advertising rules, since they create an undisclosed bias. Editorial reviews (e.g., *Publishers Weekly*) are handled differently, and it's permissible to pay for those.

>>> When advertising, you have some license to exaggerate your claims under a doctrine called "mere puffery." You can still have flair in your advertisements and on your website. What you don't want to do is lie to people, or make promises you can't keep.

### Disclaimers

Certain types of content require disclaimers. If you write nonfiction that touches on health, weight loss, law, finance, income, or any other specialized field (a rule of thumb is, it's specialized if professionals are licensed), you will probably need to include legal disclaimers. Testimonials sometimes also trigger a disclaimer requirement.

The disclaimer should state that the book is for informational or educational purposes, that it doesn't constitute professional advice, that no professional relationship is created, that described results are not typical, and that readers should consult a qualified professional for their specific situation. You've already seen one of these; I have one at the front of this book. For a deeper dive on finding sample disclaimers, download my *Beyond the Basics* resource guide.

A disclaimer is not a magic shield. If you are writing in one of these areas, get professional advice before you publish. The FTC has a long history of prosecuting marketers who make income or health claims, especially.

## Terms of Service and Refund Policies

Small businesses routinely underestimate the importance of Terms of Service on their websites. So I'm here to tell you, your terms of service are a contract you have with customers who use your website or, more importantly, who purchase products and services off your website.

Good templates exist for terms of service to ensure you comply with various internet security and forum laws. If your website is only for viewing, then a reputable template with your review will suffice. But if you sell, then you need a clear sales and refund policies are both a legal safeguard and a customer service tool. It should state plainly whether and when refunds are available, any conditions or time limits, and how a buyer requests one. My resource guide will point you in the right direction for creating terms and policies for your website.

Except in certain regulated industries with mandatory "cool off" periods, or sometimes when selling internationally, refunds are not required by law. Guarantees are also not required, and your terms of service should disclaim implied warranties.

I still think refunds are good practice to avoid chargebacks and poor reviews. But that's just my opinion. Make a business decision that works for you. Whatever you choose, make sure you honor it. Also note, as you evolve your business and update your terms, the one in effect at the time of purchase is the one you have to honor for that transaction. So keep revision records.

>>> When you sell on marketplaces like Amazon or use Merchants of Record, their terms of service will apply to the transaction. Your website terms do not override the terms of the responsible seller.

### Content and Warnings Aimed at Protecting Children

In the United States, several states have recently passed laws aimed at preventing access to pornography by minors. They are pretty strict, requiring verification of age before a user can access explicit content. Laws also exist that regulate sellers of certain controlled substances, like alcohol or cannabis.

If you write explicit or mature content, you need to think about who is accessing it and whether you are required to block access by minors. The minimum prudent practice for adult content on your own site is to gate it behind an age confirmation pop-up and to label it clearly.

A separate emerging set of requirements focuses on whether a website is likely to attract children and how their information is stored and used. The federal Children's Online Privacy Protection Act (COPPA) has long required special protections for websites that knowingly collect personal information from children under thirteen, including explicit parental consent before data collection and strict limits on how that data is used. If your site in any way targets or attracts younger readers—middle grade, young adult, or educational content—COPPA compliance is not optional.

California has been aggressive in extending child protection into the digital space. The California Age-Appropriate Design Code Act requires that online services likely to be accessed by children default to the highest privacy settings, avoid design features that manipulate or harm children, and limit the data they collect or share. Because California's rules tend to set the standard nationally, as everyone selling online reaches California consumers, best practices require you to comply with their laws.

### Privacy Policies and Data Protection

If your website collects any personal information from visitors, including through contact forms or newsletter sign-ups, or standard cookies and analytics trackers, you need a privacy policy. This is a legal requirement.

A privacy policy is a public statement of what information you collect, how you use it, whether you share it and with whom, and what choices visitors have. Several states mandate privacy disclosures for sites that collect personal data from their residents, and comprehensive state privacy statutes—again led by California—grant consumers the right to know what is collected and to request deletion.

It is not impermissible to collect and sell consumer data. Some of the biggest companies in the world do this constantly (**cough** Meta). But consumers generally hate it, so most small businesses opt out of selling their customer's information and say so in their privacy policy.

Here's what matters: *actually do what your privacy policy says.* A privacy policy that promises you don't share data while your site is piping it to advertising networks and affiliates is worse than no policy at all, because it adds a false representation on top of the compliance failure. Keep it honest, keep it current, and update it at least yearly to ensure it still accurately describes your practices.

> >>> Many website builders and email platforms generate basic privacy policy templates that you can customize. This is fine as a starting point. But read it before you publish it. A template that doesn't reflect what your site actually does is not compliant.

**Cookie Laws and GDPR for International Readers**

Speaking of privacy and data collection, if your audience includes people in Europe or the United Kingdom, the General Data Protection Regulation (GDPR) applies to how you handle their personal data, even though you're not located there. You are likely familiar with the GDPR already because it's responsible for the ubiquitous cookie banners on everyone's websites.

The GDPR sets demanding standards: a lawful basis for processing personal data, specific and genuine consent where consent is the basis, and meaningful transparency about what you actually do with the data you collect. Since cookies are the primary way websites collect and track user data, the GDPR now requires affirmative consent to be sought and recorded.

The GDPR is complicated. I tried to read it once and decided my life was too precious. Suffice to say, most website templates have GDPR-compliant banners that you can turn on. You can also find plugins that do the same thing. The sensible baseline is a privacy policy that addresses those EU/UK readers, a cookie notice, honest newsletter opt-ins without pre-checked boxes or dark patterns, and processes that honor a reader's request to see or delete their data.

### Payment Processing and PCI Compliance

When you accept card payments, you become subject to the Payment Card Industry Data Security Standard—PCI compliance, in industry shorthand. This is a set of security requirements imposed by the card networks on everyone who handles cardholder data. Among other things, PCI compliance requires annual recertification.

The good news is that you can sidestep this entirely by doing one simple thing: never touch the sensitive data yourself. When you use a reputable payment processor (Stripe, PayPal, etc.) or a hosted checkout or Merchant of Record, the customer's card information flows directly to the processor, which is built to handle it securely. You don't see their banking information, and you don't keep it in your records. This is one of the strongest practical reasons to run payments through an established processor rather than trying to build your own checkout.

Processors have features that allow you to recharge cards for customers, including for recurrent subscriptions. The processor uses an encrypted token that allows you to connect and run transactions. There's no reason for you to hold customer's banking information yourself.

>>> **Do not store customers' credit card numbers or bank information.** Storing card data turns you into a target for hackers and balloons both your security obligations and your exposure. If the data you hold is ever breached, the notice and cure requirements could bankrupt your business.

### Email Marketing and CAN-SPAM Compliance

In the United States, the CAN-SPAM Act requires that marketing emails use honest subject lines and header information, identify themselves as commercial, include a valid physical mailing address, and offer a straightforward way to unsubscribe that you honor promptly. The physical address requirement is one reason the privacy strategies from Chapter 1—a registered agent address or a virtual mailbox—are useful beyond just protecting your home address on state filings. Those same addresses satisfy the email law requirement without broadcasting where you live to your entire list.

In the United States, people do not have to opt-in to your email list before you email them. You literally cold email people, although you should think hard about whether this is a good idea. And if your list includes international subscribers, stricter rules apply. European privacy laws require genuine prior consent before you email someone—not "they gave me their email once for a different reason" consent, but actual, specific opt-in. Canada's anti-spam law is even stricter about consent and identification.

The practical path through all of this is the same path that good email platforms are built around: collect subscribers through honest opt-ins, identify yourself clearly in every message, include your address and an easy unsubscribe link, and remove people promptly when they ask (automations can handle this). And don't add them back in later without their clear consent, because that is annoying and will draw spam complaints.

Reputable email service providers bake international requirements into their tools. Use them. Emailing readers from a Gmail account is not a newsletter strategy. There's a reason spammers use Gmail. Also, email marketing software will have better deliverability. Google and Microsoft email servers (e.g. anything that goes through Outlook and Gmail, regardless of domain—which is the vast majority of email in America) determine whether a particular email should be delivered to junk mail or an inbox based on reputation. Domains with good opt-in practices tied to reputable marketing email service providers are far more likely to land in inboxes.

>>> Purchased email lists are usually a waste of money and likely to land you in junk folders or a slew of spam complaints. Too many spam complaints risk getting your domain blacklisted and your email account canceled.

### Affiliate Disclosure Requirements

If you earn income through affiliate links, such as by recommending books, tools, or services through tracked links that pay a commission when someone buys, you must let your audience know. It typically won't hurt your sales to be upfront about it, and honesty is the best policy.

The FTC requires that you disclose your financial motive clearly and conspicuously, close to the relevant recommendation, in language your audience can understand. The disclosure has to be where people will actually see it, using normal fonts. A standard disclaimer reads: "This post contains affiliate links, which means I may earn a commission at no extra cost to you."

### Website Accessibility

The Americans with Disabilities Act requires that places of public accommodation be accessible to people with disabilities. This applies to websites, not just physical spaces. This is not an abstract risk that only applies to large businesses with well-trafficked websites. Over 5,000 digital accessibility lawsuits were filed in 2025 alone, a 37 percent increase over the year before.

What does accessibility mean? The practical highlights are: the ability to navigate your site using only a keyboard, alternative text for images, captions for videos, sufficient color contrast between text and background, and readable, logically structured content. Most of this is handled at the design and template level, which means your choice of website platform matters. Major platforms like Squarespace, Wix, and WordPress have accessibility-focused themes and settings. These are more likely to be compliant than a plugin that claims to make your existing site accessible.

Early in the development process, run your site through a free accessibility checker. Fix what it flags, starting with missing alt text on images, which is the most common and easiest violation to correct. Make sure any videos you embed have captions. Choose a high-contrast theme. If you sell directly, make sure your checkout flow is keyboard-navigable. For more information on where to find these checkers, download my resources guide.

>>> The IRS offers a Disabled Access Credit for small businesses that spend money on accessibility improvements, for a maximum credit of $5,000. If you have to update your website to make it compliant, ask your CPA whether you qualify for the credit.

**Action Steps: Building Your Compliance Foundation**

1. Get a privacy policy on your site and add a cookie notice.

2. Draft terms of service and a refund policy.

3. If you write adult content, consider whether an “Over 18” gate is needed.

4. Set up your shopping car with an established payment processor. Confirm you are never storing card or bank data yourself.

5. Review your marketing copy. Is every claim accurate? Are urgency and scarcity tactics real? Are endorsements and reviews genuine? Are your promises clear?

6. If you write in a professional field or include testimonials

or affiliate links, add required disclaimers.

7. Set up your newsletter through a reputable email platform, use a non-home address for your required physical mailing address, and collect subscribers through honest opt-in only.

8. Run your website through a free accessibility checker and update it with fixes, such as missing image alt text, video captions, keyboard navigation, and strong visual contrast.

## Chapter Seven

# TORTS RELATED TO YOUR CONTENT

Most of this book concerns the business of writing. This chapter concerns the writing itself, and the rare but real ways that the words on the page can expose you to a lawsuit.

A tort is a civil wrong that causes harm to another person and gives them the right to sue for damages. For authors, the torts that may come up arise from what we publish about real people and companies, namely defamation and invasions of privacy. (I assume you already know not to plagiarize.)

I wrote this chapter because I see this question discussed a lot in author forums on social media. Most of the advice circulating among authors is incorrect. To be frank, the risk of a lawsuit, much less a judgment, is infinitesimally small for fiction writers, and small even for nonfiction writers. But because lawsuits are ruinous even if you are ultimately vindicated, it's best to avoid them altogether. So here's what you need to know to stay out of trouble when you're an author.

## Defamation and Libel

Authors deeply fear being accused of defamation if they write characters inspired by other people, or write nonfiction that is about real people and events. Many worry obsessively about whether releases are required before they publish.

Defamation is a false statement of fact, communicated to others, that injures the subject's reputation. There are two types of defamation: libel and slander. Libel is in written form, and slander is oral. The distinction between libel and slander is pedantic, and most lawyers simply refer to both as defamation.

For something to be defamatory, the statement must be a false one on an issue of fact. Truth is a complete defense. In contrast, opinions can be negative, but they are not defamatory because opinions cannot be proven true or false. But you can't escape liability for asserting a false fact about someone by dressing it up as opinion—the most obvious way being, "In my opinion ... X."

The problems usually happen when a statement is a hybrid between fact and opinion. Those are the cases that end up before juries. I'll give you a few examples to illustrate the conceptual difference.

*Fact: President Trump is eighty years old.*

*Opinion: President Trump is an ugly old man.*

*Hybrid: I think President Trump is ugly because he's dying.*

Note that I used a real, living person in this example. It is, in fact, permissible to mention real people in print sometimes. What matters is that I didn't actually make any assertions about President

Trump, but rather used his name to create an illustration. Since I am not asserting those statements as facts, they are not defamatory.

The risk to fiction authors is usually small because defamatory statements must be about an identifiable person (or company) to be actionable. Fictional characters can be inspired by real people and events without being defamatory due to lack of identifiability.

One of my best friends sometimes asks me which of my characters was inspired by her. The answer is: there are several things in my novels that are inspired by our hijinks, her mannerisms, and things she says. But no single character is *her*. Fiction is fiction.

The First Amendment also protects against defamation claims when the subject is a public figure, such as a celebrity or a politician. For a false statement about public figures to be actionable as defamation, the subject must prove that the author made it with malice, meaning they knew it was false and didn't just make it accidentally. Private individuals do not have to prove malice, however—just that you made a false statement about them and published it.

### The Fictional Character Disclaimer

So you've written a novel, and some of the characters occasionally resemble people you know in real life. Is there a foolproof way to protect yourself from getting sued?

First of all, no. In the United States, *anyone can sue you for anything at anytime*. That's a bit of an exaggeration, but not by much.

In a collective, existential cry for certainty in a litigious country, works of fiction nearly all include the following disclaimer: "This is a work of fiction. Names, characters, places, and incidents are either the product of the author's imagination or are used fictitiously. Any resemblance to actual persons, living or dead, is purely coincidental." I find this disclaimer hilarious, even though I also use it.

In 1934, MGM made the film *Rasputin and the Empress*, which was a dramatized account of the Romanov collapse and Rasputin's murder. The film included a character based on a real woman, Princess Irina Youssoupoff, who was still living at the time. The film depicted a character—clearly identifiable as her—being sexually assaulted by Rasputin. She sued for defamation and won a sizable judgment in England.

The studios panicked. They clearly talked to their lawyers because suddenly the "purely coincidental" boilerplate began appearing on films and then migrated into book publishing as standard front matter. It was essentially a defensive legal posture that became ritualized through repetition.

I include it in my novels out of performative professionalism, not because the disclaimer actually does anything. Because it actually doesn't work. Case after case has determined that the disclaimer doesn't protect you if the character is clearly identifiable as a real person despite the fictional framing. Still, to avoid looking amateurish, I recommend all authors include it.

The truth is: fiction can defame. If you create a character that a reasonable reader would identify as a real person, and you portray that person as doing or being something false and reputation-damaging, the disclaimer won't save you. The better answer is to simply not make your characters too obviously real people. And if you must—because you are writing historical fiction, for example—then make sure the people are dead at the time of publication, and that writing about them doesn't defame ongoing business concerns or living people. You can't defame the dead.

### Are Releases Required for Nonfiction to Avoid Defamation Claims?

This is where I frequently see wrong advice given on social media, so let me set the record straight: Releases are not required to publish nonfiction about real people. There is no law that says you must obtain someone's permission before writing about them. Can you imagine if that were the case? Journalists, biographers, and gossip bloggers would be paralyzed. Think of how many unauthorized biographies exist about celebrities, and you'll realize what I'm saying is true even for books.

What releases do is *reduce risk*. A signed release in which a person consents to being depicted and waives claims arising from that depiction provides some protection from later lawsuits. Although, again, releases are not foolproof—no waiver is, because certain torts cannot be waived and consideration (payment) is required. But for biographies of real people, or for your memoirs including real people, it won't hurt you to get releases.

The defamation analysis for nonfiction is the same as for fiction. Truth is your primary defense. If what you write is accurate and you can support it, a defamation claim won't succeed. This is why journalists are careful about documenting their sources. Journals, emails, texts, photographs, court records, medical records, witness corroboration—these are not just research tools; they are your evidentiary file.

For memoir authors writing about abuse, addiction, family dysfunction, or other sensitive personal history, a few principles may help. First, stick to what you actually experienced and can support. Second, ask honestly whether every private detail you're revealing is necessary to the work. Third, understand that changing someone's name alone is not sufficient protection if everything else still points directly at them. Fourth, be aware that memoirs can have personal costs and destroy relationships, and this is usually the bigger danger than a lawsuit (most people can't afford lawyers).

When the stakes are genuinely high—you're writing about someone with the means and motive to litigate, the subject matter is sensitive enough that reasonable people could disagree about what's fact or opinion, or you're making specific claims you can't corroborate with evidence other than your own testimony—a prepublication legal review could be worthwhile.

### Rights of Privacy and False Light Torts

Separate from defamation, some aspects of personal privacy are protected. Privacy torts vary considerably between states, but the general principle is that you should not publicly disclose someone else's private information when it is not of legitimate public concern. For example, it would never be appropriate to publish someone's social security number. Medical information, financial status, sexual behaviors, and criminal histories should be scrutinized. As a rule of thumb, don't be an asshole when it comes to other people.

False light is another tort that varies significantly between states, but should be considered. Portraying someone in a false light includes appropriating someone's name or likeness for commercial benefit. This comes up most frequently with authors who use celebrities in their marketing in a way that implies the celebrity endorses their work. But it can also come up when people (especially famous people) are used as characters in books, even if it is not defamatory.

It is not the case that you can never mention a celebrity or other real person, a real business, a historical event, or a real place. But if you are uncomfortable drawing conclusions about what is fair game, then the easier practice is to simply avoid it.

### Trigger Warnings: Legal Requirement or Best Practice?

Content warnings are common in independent and small-press publications. There is no legal reason a trigger or content warning is necessary. There are practical reasons, however. Some platforms require them. You also want to avoid attracting minors to adult content. Beyond those specific concerns, content warnings are best understood as a reader-relations best practice rather than a legal obligation. They set accurate expectations, can reduce complaints and refund requests, and are increasingly expected by readers in certain genres. Providing them thoughtfully is good business and good faith with your audience.

### Insurance Considerations for Authors

Once your business grows enough to have assets at risk, consider purchasing commercial liability insurance. Media liability insurance, sometimes called media perils or publisher's liability coverage, covers claims like defamation, invasion of privacy, and certain intellectual property claims. General liability and errors and omissions policies also sometimes cover these claims. When you shop for insurance, use a broker who can explain coverage differences between policies. Insurance typically covers both the cost of defending a claim, which is substantial even when you ultimately win, and any damages, up to a policy limit. It also may cover some of the other risks that come with running any small business.

**Action Steps: Protecting Yourself from Content Claims**

1. Include your fiction disclaimer, but understand that it is not protective if you create a character who is identifiable as a real person and that person is still alive.

2. If you're writing nonfiction about real people, write what's true and keep the evidence.

3. Get releases when you can, but they are not required.

4. Know the difference between public figures and private individuals. Do not hold others in false light, and that is especially the case when it comes to celebrities.

5. Otherwise, writing about public figures carry lower legal risk than private individuals. The more private your subject, the more carefully you should treat their privacy.

6. Regardless, always consider carefully before publishing anything that might be considered private and that would cause offense to reasonable people.

7. If the stakes are high, get a pre-publication legal review.

8. Consider busying business insurances, including media liability insurance.

Chapter Eight

# DEALING WITH SCAMMERS AND PREDATORS

Wherever there are people with dreams and a little money to make them come true, there are predators ready to exploit them. And the problem of scammers, pirates, and predators has only expanded thanks to the internet.

Not long ago, I watched an investigative journalist piece about a company that promised to publish and promote authors until they got movie deals for their books. These scammers were so successful in their cons that they fleeced the retirement savings out of multiple people to the tune of six figures—all the while never actually publishing the book or getting the promised industry deals. A ring of these scammers were finally arrested in San Diego and charged with crimes by the Department of Justice. But the DOJ won't be able to get back the life savings or fix the intense emotional damage done to the victims. It's just heartbreaking.

I wish that story was singular. But I know it's not. I've been publishing for three years, and I get spammy, scammy solicitations every single day. My debut novel was pirated almost immediately. And I fell victim to a famous, supposedly reputable company's scam on independent authors—which has led to legal action (they cheated the wrong author).

This chapter is a field guide to the scams that target authors, the warning signs that should make you stop, and the concrete steps to take if you are hit. The single most protective habit you can build is a healthy skepticism toward anyone who approaches you with an offer that seems designed to flatter your ambition while emptying your wallet. Avoiding scammers and predatory marketers is the best defense.

It's harder to avoid pirates, and everyone suffers from them. Chapter 12 is devoted to the problem of piracy that plagues authors.

### Common Scams Targeting Authors

**Vanity publishing and fake publishing deals** are the oldest traps in the business. A company presents itself as a selective publisher and tells you your manuscript has been chosen, then reveals that you must pay thousands of dollars for editing, design, marketing, and production. A legitimate traditional publisher pays you; it does not ask you to pay it. Paid publishing services can be honest when they are transparent about being a service you hire, but a company that disguises a paid service as a competitive acquisition is misleading you, and the contracts often grab your rights as well as your cash. Buyer beware.

**Free ISBNs** lure authors who do not yet understand that whoever is listed as the ISBN's registrant is the publisher of record. Sometimes this doesn't matter—Amazon isn't going to keep your rights if you decide to remove your book from KDP. But others will have rights buried in their terms and then force you to buy them out to get your work back. Owning your own ISBNs keeps that control in your hands. Once I got serious about being an author, I bought a package of 100 ISBNs from Bowker because the marginal cost is much cheaper in bulk, and I own and control every single piece of writing I publish.

>>> Every new edition of your work requires its own ISBN. For print books, you cannot so much as change the color of the paper from white to cream without a new ISBN, although you can re-cover it. You also need an ISBN for each format: paperback, ebook, audiobook, hardcover.

**Fake book award schemes** sell prestige. You receive word that your book is a finalist for an award you never entered, followed by a request for an entry fee, a gala ticket, or a payment for a sticker and certificate. Real awards exist, but be wary of any award that materializes out of nowhere and exists mainly to collect fees from the authors it flatters.

**Plagiarism and stolen work** run in both directions. Scammers scrape and republish books under alternative names to collect royalties, and they steal cover art and descriptions.

**Fake royalty and advance scams** dangle money to extract money. You are told a royalty or advance awaits, but first you must pay a processing fee, a tax, or a deposit to release it. No legitimate payer requires you to send money in order to receive money.

**Predatory marketing services** promise to make your book a bestseller through guaranteed placements, manufactured rankings, or vague promotional packages priced far above their value. They prey on the hardest problem authors face—visibility—and they rarely deliver anything that remotely justifies the cost.

**Fake review services** offer to sell you reviews, which not only wastes money but violates the terms of service of every major retailer. Buying reviews can get your account suspended and your books removed, turning a marketing expense into a catastrophe.

### Red Flags: What to Watch For

Scams vary, but the warning signs are consistent, and learning them helps you recognize new frauds as they emerge, because fraudsters are remarkably creative and AI is making them harder to recognize.

Spammers sometimes assume the identities of famous authors, book clubs, and legitimate services. AI makes their emails more fluent in English, so they are getting harder to spot. But if it comes from a free email service like Gmail, or it defies common sense that a famous author is sending you a cold email, it's baloney.

You may have the soul of an artist, but when it comes to book vendors and marketers, keep the mind of a cynic. Be deeply skeptical of guarantees that sound too good to be true. Legitimate professionals promise effort and competence, not guaranteed bestseller status or specific sales numbers. Most promotion services that offer to list your book on their social media platforms are padded with bots and won't give you the results you want to see.

Treat unsolicited offers and out-of-the-blue emails and social media messages with suspicion, especially when they congratulate you effusively before getting to the ask. Scrutinize any arrangement built around high upfront fees, particularly when they approach you as though you've been selected for a prestigious honor.

Resist pressure to decide quickly, since urgency is a manipulation tactic designed to stop you from researching or thinking. Refuse requests for sensitive personal information, passwords, or account credentials, which no legitimate partner needs. And watch for fake publisher websites and copycat brands that imitate the name and look of a reputable company closely enough to fool a hurried glance.

I'm unwilling to pay anyone for promotions or reviews who come to me unsolicited. I usually delete their messages unanswered or flag them as junk. But sometimes people get through. Recently, I was messaged by a longtime follower on Instagram who told me they loved my latest novel and wanted to post a review about it. I responded they are welcome to do so, but that I don't pay for reviews. They responded back, "Well I just wasted my precious time!" It was so crazy that I took a screenshot and shared it with my friends—and then blocked them.

### Financial Scams

This is advice for anyone, not just authors: never wire money to someone you don't know. And only wire money using instructions you've verified with the recipient directly—preferably twice. The most dangerous scammers use wires to commit fraud because a completed wire is extremely difficult to claw back.

The same logic drives demands for payment in cryptocurrency, which is fast, irreversible, and hard to trace, making it a favorite of scammers and a reason to be alarmed when anyone insists on it.

Fake bank transfers and counterfeit checks run the trick in reverse: you receive a check or a transfer that looks real, you are asked to refund part of it or forward funds, and days later the original payment bounces, leaving you out the money you sent.

Authors also face chargeback fraud as sellers. That's where a buyer obtains your product and then disputes the charge to get their money back while keeping the product. It's annoying, but you should just expect a small percentage of loss in business to customer theft, no different from retail stores suffering shoplifting and breakage.

Finally, tax and corporate filing scams purporting to come from official agencies use threats of arrest or immediate penalties to panic you into paying. Remember that tax authorities initiate contact by mail and do not demand instant payment by gift card, wire, or cryptocurrency. The status of your LLC and any due filings can be checked online with your state at any time.

Business owners are frequently targeted for both tax and corporate filing scams. I've had scammers call me and claim that my business is about to get levied if I didn't pay taxes to them right away. And I've received fake "official" mail demanding I pay bills for copier ink I never bought or file documents with the Secretary of State that weren't needed.

### Protecting Your Accounts

Your publishing and financial accounts are the keys to your business, and protecting them is mostly about a few disciplined habits. Using password manager software, create strong, unique passwords for every account so that a breach of one service does not unlock the others. Enable two-factor authentication everywhere it is offered, because that second step blocks the great majority of account takeovers even when a password is stolen.

Two-factor authentication is strongest when it is biometric (like passkeys that require face scans or fingerprints) or uses an authenticator app, like Google Authenticator. Text messages and emails for 2FA are more vulnerable to spoofing and hackers, who use them to get into your devices and steal everything you own. I have been involved in litigation against major telecommunications companies for exactly these types of breaches, so I know this is a real thing that happens.

Also learn to recognize social engineering, in which an attacker manipulates you into revealing information or granting access by impersonating someone you trust, and phishing emails, which mimic legitimate platforms and lure you to fake login pages designed to capture your credentials. Before you ever enter a password, confirm that you reached the site by navigating there yourself rather than by clicking a link in an unexpected message.

Protecting your pen names and brand means watching for impersonators who set up fake author pages or social accounts in your name to deceive your readers. I have had my identity as a lawyer spoofed to "recommend" financial products, which required effort on my part to get removed, and I didn't need to be famous for this to happen. The way I found this out is that I keep a Google Alert set up for my name, pen names, and business names.

I also watch out for other authors. When I see spoofed accounts misappropriating another author's identity, I will report it and notify the real author. As a community, we can work together to fight against the scammers.

### What to Do If You're Targeted

If a scammer reaches or harms you, acting promptly limits the damage and helps others avoid the same trap. Report the fraud to the relevant platform first, since retailers and social media platforms such as Amazon and Meta have mechanisms to address impersonation, fake listings, and abuse. This is, in fact, in your interest. Because if your identity gets entangled with a scammer, you may see your legitimate accounts shut down, and getting this fixed disrupts your business and is slow and frustrating.

Report serious fraud and theft to law enforcement, including your local police, your state attorney general, and the appropriate federal channels for internet crime (usually the FBI), which is also often necessary documentation for disputing fraudulent charges. File complaints with the consumer protection authorities, including the Federal Trade Commission, and with the Better Business Bureau, which help build a record against the bad actor even when they cannot recover your money directly. Don't be disappointed if law enforcement doesn't do anything right away. It often takes several complaints before they devote resources to capturing and prosecuting a scammer, and you're helping to build their files.

If you have exposed financial information, move to protect your credit by alerting your bank and card issuers, watching your statements, and considering a fraud alert or credit freeze with the credit bureaus to stop someone from opening accounts in your name. Where the harm involves a website or a payment, report it to the payment processor, the platform, and the web host involved, since these intermediaries can freeze funds, remove content, or terminate the bad actor's account. Acting quickly and documenting everything as you go gives you the best chance of containing the harm and supporting any later effort to recover.

### Getting Refunds and Chargebacks

When you have paid a scammer or a service that failed to deliver, recovering your money follows a ladder of escalating options. Start by demanding a refund directly and in writing, stating clearly what you paid for, what went wrong, and the refund you expect, because a clear written demand sometimes works and always creates a record. If that fails and you paid by card or through a service like PayPal, dispute the charge with your card issuer or the platform, which is exactly why paying by credit card rather than by wire or cryptocurrency matters so much: card payments come with built-in dispute rights that irreversible methods do not.

If all of that fails, you can consider legal action. But go in clear-eyed about the obstacles. Small claims court is designed for modest disputes and can be pursued without a lawyer, but it has dollar limits. And even if you get a judgment, it must still be collected. The hardest barrier for most suits is jurisdiction: many scammers operate from other states or other countries, beyond the practical reach of a small claims court, which is precisely why prevention and reversible payment methods matter so much.

My *Beyond the Basics* guide includes frequently asked questions on how to deal with disputes that are tilting toward litigation and provides links to useful resources.

## Action Steps: Protecting Yourself from Scammers and Predators

1. Build your skepticism muscle now, before you need it. The single best protection against scams is knowing they exist and what they look like, so you're not caught up in one.

2. Remember the fundamental rule of legitimate publishing: money flows to the author, not from the author. Pay to play is suspect.

3. Buy your own ISBNs from Bowker.

4. Before you pay any marketing or promotional service, do your due diligence. Avoid engaging with inbound solicitations, as the vast majority are scams.

5. Never pay a fee to receive money. Royalties, advances, prizes, grants, and contest winnings do not require you to send payment first.

6. Use a password manager and two-factor authentication.

7. Never wire money to a vendor you don't personally know, and treat any insistence on wire transfer or cryptocurrency as a serious warning sign.

8. Set up Google Alerts for your author name and your pen names. You want to know if someone is impersonating you online.

9. If you are hit, report to the platform, report to law enforcement, alert your bank and card issuers, and document everything. Speed matters for limiting damage and for building the record you'll need if any recovery routes are available.

10. Pay by credit card for any significant vendor relationship. Chargebacks are not glamorous, but they are real leverage. Wires and crypto are not easily to recover.

11. If you get a suspicious official-looking notice or call about your LLC, your taxes, or your business filings, verify it directly with the agency. Also, agencies do not demand immediate payment by gift card, wire, or cryptocurrency.

12. Tell other authors what you see. We're a community and authors routinely help each other.

# PART III

## INTELLECTUAL PROPERTY FOUNDATIONS

ACID SQUIRREL MEDIA LLC

Chapter Nine

# COPYRIGHT FUNDAMENTALS

A few years ago, I presented *Legal Basics for Authors* as a workshop at the Romance Writers of America annual conference. The discussion was heavily dominated by copyright questions. I suspect that's because copyright is at the heart of every author's business.

Copyright is the property right that makes your work an asset with value that you can sell, license, and even bequeath. As authors, we value the work we put into our writing; and as such, we value the copyrights of other writers, musicians, and artists. It is therefore no surprise that AI has especially offended the author community because of its disrespect of copyright.

### What Copyright Does and Doesn't Protect

Copyright protects original creative works fixed in a tangible form. For authors, that means the text you put on paper (or screen). But it applies to creative works in all formats, including books, but also your blogs and websites and articles. Copyright also applies to other types of creative works, like music and visual and graphic arts.

While copyright protects your particular expression, it does not protect the underlying ideas, facts, or concepts in your works. You own the specific words and the creative way you arranged them. But you cannot copyright a plot premise, a theme, a historical fact, a method, or a stock character type, all of which remain free for other authors to use.

Copyright also does not protect names, titles, and short phrases, which is why a book title is generally not protected by copyright, though it may be possible to trademark it (which is a distinct law explained in Chapter 11). Understanding this line clarifies both what you can defend in your own work and what you are free to draw on from others.

You don't have to register your copyright for protection to attach. It is automatic from the moment you fix your original work in tangible form, e.g. by typing words into a document. You do not have to file with the US Copyright Office first, and you do not have to mail yourself a copy or write any magic words to claim it. You don't need to use the copyright symbol (that's the little c in a circle), either. Marking things as copyrighted and noting the year the work was first created can be useful for public notice, is not a bad idea, however.

If you choose to register your work with the US Copyright Office, you can easily do it by filling out a form online. It is easy, and you do not need a service or a lawyer to do it for you. The USCO increased the filing fees to $85 per work in 2026 (up from $45) set to take place in late fall or early winter 2026. Also, be advised that if your work includes a print version, then you are supposed to mail two hard copies to the Library of Congress as part of the registration.

When you're ready to invest the time and fees, registration is worth doing. Federal copyright registration gives you advantages that automatic common law copyright alone does not. It increases your legal options and available damages, including the option to sue in federal court, which makes your copyright easier to enforce. But it is not unusual for authors to wait to register their works until their businesses are established.

### How Using AI Impacts Your Copyrights

If you're using AI to write your words for you, there's a pretty significant risk that those words are not copyright protected. This is a legal area that is rapidly evolving, so bear that in mind—this book may need an update pretty quickly!

The basic principle, however, is that copyright protects *human* authorship, not machine authorship. Material generated by AI, without meaningful human creative control, is generally not going to be protected by copyright because it lacks the essential creativity. A work combining human-authored writing with AI-generated portions *may* still be protected as to the parts *you* authored. If you're using AI to generate your written work, even in part, then you may be at risk of having your book copied and resold, and you won't have recourse.

### Work-for-Hire

If you write words for others—you're a copywriter, technical writer, ghostwriter, or create commissioned pieces—the question of who owns the copyright will come up. Normally, the person who creates a work owns its copyright, which means you own what you write. But work-for-hire is the major exception. Under that doctrine, the copyright belongs not to the creator, but to the party who commissioned it or employed the creator.

A common example is employment at a job. If you work for an employer and get paid a wage, anything you create for the employer belongs to the employer. That's why some employers have you sign "Invention Assignment Agreements." But even without such an agreement, if they hired you to write something, they own it by default. If you want to own the rights to what you write on contract for another, you will need to negotiate it and put it in writing.

### Public Domain

Very old works eventually go into the public domain, which means they can be copied by anyone. A copyright written by an individual author currently endures for the author's lifetime plus seventy years. A work by a group of authors continues for seventy years past the death of the last surviving author. Works-for-hire, anonymous works, and works owned by corporations have a copyright of 95 years from publication or 120 years from creation, whichever expires first. Works can also enter the public domain when the creator does so voluntarily (e.g., open-source software) or by failing to enforce their copyright.

This tells you two things. First, your body of work can be inherited by your estate after your death, making it a valuable commodity. You can also use it as collateral and bank, sell, and trade against your intellectual property.

Second: you can use old works as part of your work (or even reprint public domain works wholesale, which happened a lot in the early years of Kindle) without a license. For example, as a general matter, you can quote *The Bible* because it was written thousands of years ago. It is in the public domain. You can also record and use music written by Mozart on your website. You can re-tell old folktales and fairy tales, too.

There is a caveat: modern translations, revisions, and performances (like by a philharmonic playing Mozart) are themselves copyrighted works. That's why you can re-tell the story *The Little Mermaid*, but you can't use elements of Disney's version or its artwork. You can probably give your little mermaid red hair, but you're going to run into trouble if you name her Ariel and she has a crab bestie named Sebastian.

The public domain question comes up most when cultural touchstones, like when the lyrics to the song "Happy Birthday to You" are used in a novel or a movie. I used that specific song on purpose: for years, a corporation enforced a hefty licensing fee for using that song anywhere, from movies to restaurants. That changed in 2016 when a court determined that they held the copyright to a specific piano version of the song, but not the song itself. So now restaurants can sing it instead of their weird, made-up versions.

### International Copyright Considerations

An international treaty framework means that most countries extend copyright protection to works by authors from other member countries automatically, without requiring you to register separately in each nation. Your work is therefore generally protected in many countries under each country's particular laws. That said, the details of protection, the available remedies, and the practical difficulty of enforcement vary considerably from country to country. More importantly, pursuing an infringer overseas is so difficult as to be impractical for a small business or independent author. So, yes, your copyright is not confined to your own country, but that won't stop pirates.

## Copyright Infringement and Licenses

Infringement occurs when someone copies, distributes, or makes derivatives of your copyrighted work without permission (and without a defense like fair use). When it happens, copyright law provides civil remedies that you pursue through a lawsuit. A court can order the infringer to stop through an injunction. You can also recover your actual damages plus the infringer's profits attributable to the infringement. Alternatively—and this is where federal registration pays off—you may elect statutory damages instead, and you may recover your attorneys' fees. Because litigation is expensive, the availability of statutory damages and fee recovery often determines whether suing an infringer is economically realistic.

Owning a copyright means you control who may use the work and how, and you exercise that control through licenses. A license is an agreement giving someone permission to use your work. The terms are negotiated, and a license can be exclusive or non-exclusive. They can also be limited in use (e.g. commercial or non-commercial), duration, territory, medium, or format. For example, you can grant a license that is just for audio, or just for the Spanish translation, or just for sale in Europe. Licenses and transfers of copyright generally must be in writing.

When you work with a literary agent, publisher, or a distributor (including, importantly, Amazon), you are entering a licensing relationship. An agent does not buy your copyright but represents you in licensing it to publishers. A distributor takes your work to retail channels under terms that define the rights you are granting, the territories and formats covered, the duration, and the share each side keeps. It's important to understand the terms you are agreeing to when you license your work to anyone else—even when they are not negotiable terms.

Licensing runs in the other direction too. You will come across this most often when you use images for covers, marketing, and articles. Other artwork to think about: fonts, memes, flourishes like scrolls and filigrees, icons, and emojis. Copyright also covers other people's text, music, and lyrics—even shorter works like poetry and micro-blogs. When you use third-party material with permission, you are doing so subject to a license from the owner, and your scope of use is defined by that license.

Many licenses (especially when given for free) are limited to non-commercial uses, or in types of reproductions, so you need to understand what you are bargaining for. Stock images you purchase usually come with standard, perpetual commercial licenses that allow you to use the image in publishing in books and online; but they may restrict you from, say, printing the image on a T-shirt. They may require attribution (especially when used for blogging or articles—less often on websites).

Another trap for the unwary: celebrity images. When a photo is taken of a famous person (or anyone, actually), that image's copyright is owned by the photographer. But the famous person also has a right of publicity. What that means is that famous people's faces are their commercial commodity, and they control how it is used. That means an image of a famous person can be used for newsworthy publications (like how journalists use them), but not on a commercial product (like a website selling face cream) without the famous person's permission.

Another area of frequent concern: What if you alter the image? Who owns the copyright? The answer is that the original copyright holder owns the copyright to the element you used, and you still must license it before creating the derivative work. But the final artwork—presuming you made enough changes that it is distinct—belongs to you. So if you use several elements on Canva to build a book cover, the elements you used are under a commercial license, but the final cover belongs to you.

Bottom line: Using copyrighted works beyond what their licenses allow is infringement, even if you paid for it. Keep records of the licenses you get so you can prove your rights to use each element, and when in doubt about whether your intended use is covered, confirm before you publish rather than after a complaint arrives.

**Action Steps: Protecting and Managing Your Copyrights**

1. Understand what copyright protects and what it does not. Your specific words and creative expression are protected. Ideas, facts, plot premises, themes, stock character types, titles, and short phrases are not.

2. Know that copyright protection is automatic the moment you fix your work in tangible form. You do not need

to file anything, mail yourself a copy, or use the copyright symbol to own your copyright.

3. Register your work with the US Copyright Office when your business is established enough to justify the cost. Registration unlocks federal court access, statutory damages, and the possibility of recovering attorneys' fees, all of which make enforcement economically realistic.

4. If you use AI to generate any portion of your written work, understand that those portions may not be copyright protected.

5. If you write for hire, get clarity on ownership in writing before you start. If you want to own what you create on contract, negotiate it upfront.

6. Keep records of every image, font, music clip, and other third-party asset you use, along with the license that covers your use. When your intended use is not clearly covered, confirm before you publish.

7. You own the copyright of your derivative or altered works, but you must license the elements.

8. Be careful with celebrity images. The photographer owns the copyright to the photo, but the subject controls the commercial use of their likeness. Both matter.

9. When you sign with an agent, publisher, or distributor, read the licensing terms. You are granting specific rights,

and you need to know which ones, for how long, and in what territories and formats.

10. Your copyright is an asset you can sell, license, or trade on, and your estate can inherit it.

# Chapter Ten

# Fair Use and Plagiarism

Sometimes you can use the works of others without a license. The question is, when is that use "fair use" and when is it infringement or plagiarism? Plagiarism, by the way, is not the same thing as copyright infringement, although the two ideas are constantly confused.

## The Plagiarism Threshold: How Much Is Too Much?

Plagiarism is the act of presenting someone else's work or ideas as your own without credit. You can do this without committing a copyright infringement. For example, if you published the public domain version of *Romeo and Juliet* as your own work instead of crediting William Shakespeare, you have committed plagiarism.

Plagiarism is unethical because it is fraudulent to claim someone else's labor as your own. But it is mainly enforced as an ethical standard by communities, schools, and readers, rather than by courts. This comes up most frequently in academics, which can cause legal issues under education law—but education law is outside the scope of this book. (If you need help in this area, I also publish a series of books on education law with another lawyer that are available for purchase.) In general, the standard for plagiarism is strict about attribution: cite your sources and never pass off another's words or ideas as your own. Plagiarism is just plain wrong, and citing your sources isn't that hard.

### The First-Sale Doctrine Is Not a License to Copy

A related misconception worth clearing up, especially for older people who grew up using physical media: buying a book, album, or piece of artwork does not give you the right to reproduce it. What you purchase is a copy of the work, not the copyright itself. The first-sale doctrine permits you to resell, lend, or give away your physical copy, which is why used bookstores and libraries can operate legally. It does not permit you to scan the book and post it online, reproduce passages in your own publication, or make any other copies. Ownership of a copy and ownership of reproduction rights are entirely different things.

### Fair Use Doctrine: The Four-Factor Test

Returning to copyrights: Fair use is the doctrine that permits limited use of copyrighted material without permission in certain circumstances. Fair use is not a fixed rule but a flexible standard, decided case by case by weighing four factors together, with no single factor decisive. There's no "safe harbor" word count where a short phrase turns into an infringement, and you should also know that the widely circulated belief that you can quote up to 300 words (or any other specific number) without permission is a myth.

The first factor is the purpose and character of your use, including whether it is commercial (you are using it in business, to make money, etc.). Even in some commercial applications, it may be fair use to repeat another's words or art if your use is transformative, meaning whether you have added new meaning, message, or purpose rather than merely reproducing the original. Commentary, criticism, parody, and scholarship are classic transformative uses, and often will be fair uses. That's not the same thing as repeating the words in your novel (such as song lyrics or movie quotes) without critical or academic commentary, even if attributed, because that is purely commercial and not transformative.

The second factor is the nature of the original work, with creative works such as novels and poems receiving stronger protection than factual works. Quoting from a fictional work is generally riskier than quoting from a factual one. The reason is that underlying facts, ideas, and concepts cannot be copyrighted.

The third factor is the amount and substantiality of what you used, both in quantity and in importance, so taking a small portion favors fair use, while taking the heart of a work can weigh against it even if the portion is short. Importantly, common words and phrases cannot be copyrighted. So merely using words that appear in other works, especially if they are short phrases or phrases in the public lexicon, does not support an infringement claim. For example, just because "I'll be back," was used by Arnold Schwarzenegger in *Terminator* doesn't mean the phrase "I'll be back," by itself is copyright protected. The words in that order are in common use. To be protected, the copied work still must be original work.

The fourth factor is the effect on the market for the original, asking whether your use harms the copyright owner's ability to profit or substitutes for the original, which courts treat as especially significant. Some cases successfully argue that a repeat of a work has not harmed the copyright owner—or even better for the defense, has served only to help the owner profit. But while this can be a viable argument, it is still best to avoid the lawsuit in the first place.

Because these factors are weighed together and applied to specific facts, judgment and experience are required when determining whether something is fair use—and even then, there are no guarantees. Fair use is a defense that you raise and potentially have to prove. Accordingly, it is subject to the vagaries of litigation, judges, and juries. Which is why, when in doubt, get permission.

## Derivative Works

In the last chapter, I mentioned book covers that use Canva elements as derivative work—you must license the original elements even though the newly arranged artwork belongs to you. To define it further, a derivative work is an original work based on someone else's copyrighted original: a sequel using another author's characters, an adaptation of a novel into a screenplay, a retelling that borrows the specific creative expression of a source work, or fan fiction that incorporates protected elements. Creating a derivative work requires permission from the original copyright holder unless fair use applies, and fair use is a much harder argument to make when the borrowing is extensive and the new work competes in the same market as the original.

This is distinct from drawing inspiration, which is always permitted. Copyright does not protect ideas, themes, or plot premises.

You can write a story about a boy who discovers he has magical powers and attends a school for wizards. But you cannot write a sequel about Hogwarts because you cannot copy specific characters, settings, dialogue, and creative expression from *Harry Potter* without a license (that is unlikely to be granted in that case). The line between inspiration and derivation is not always bright. The question is whether you have borrowed protected expression or merely a general concept; and when the answer is the former, you need a license.

Fan fiction occupies a legally complicated space. Most major rights holders tolerate it when it is non-commercial (e.g., you aren't blogging it for money on Wattpad or packaging it into a book), and it's clearly labeled. But tolerance is not foolproof, and permission may be withdrawn or the use challenged. More importantly, if you are writing fan fiction with any commercial intent, you are inviting liability.

### Using Quotes, Song Lyrics, and Movie References

This comes up most often in fiction, creative non-fiction, and copywriting: using song lyrics and movie or television quotes. Large music publishers are notoriously aggressive about enforcement, song lyrics are short so even a single line can represent a substantial portion of the whole work, and quoting even a few words of a song in your book can draw a demand for a license or a takedown. The safe practice with lyrics is to seek permission or simply not quote them, since you can almost always evoke a song by referring to its title and artist, which are not protected by copyright, rather than reproducing the lyrics themselves.

Movies and television are a little easier because titles, character names, and the bare fact that a film or show exists are generally not protected by copyright. A character watching a well-known movie, mentioning it by name, or reacting to its content is typically fine. Reproducing actual dialogue or extended passages from a screenplay, however, uses protected expression and can infringe just as quoting a book would. The reliable pattern across all of these is that referring to the existence of a cultural work, by name and creator, is safe, while reproducing the protected words within it is risky.

So you may think, *Okay, I'll just paraphrase*. Paraphrasing can work, but it needs to be genuine rephrasing. Restating someone's ideas or facts in your own words is generally fine because ideas and facts are not protected. A paraphrase that captures a concept without copying the expression avoids infringement. The trap is close paraphrasing, where you change a few words while tracking the original's structure, phrasing, and distinctive choices so closely that you have really copied the expression in light disguise (e.g., "Be, or not be, that is the query," is not a safe paraphrasing of *Hamlet*, even for Yoda). Close paraphrasing is still infringement because copyright protects the expression and not merely the exact words.

Attribution, as noted above, addresses the ethics of plagiarism but does not by itself make copying lawful. So the sound practice is to truly transform what you borrow into your own expression when you paraphrase, to credit your sources for ethical reasons, and to recognize that neither paraphrasing nor crediting substitutes for permission when you are using a substantial amount of someone's actual protected expression.

## AI, Fair Use, and Your Copyrights

As noted in Chapter 9, AI raises significant copyright issues that are still being resolved by the courts. The headline drawing litigation currently comes from authors who sued AI companies such as OpenAI and Anthropic for using their works to train AI without permission. Some settlements have already paid out to those authors, and the AI companies claim they are no longer engaging in the practice. But numerous lawsuits are still pending, with authors and publishers arguing that ingesting copyrighted works to train a commercial AI system is not fair use. As professional writers whose work may one day be fed into AI machines, is an area worth monitoring, and professional author organizations have been active in advocating for authors' interests. Be aware, also, whether drafts you are sticking into AI for editing or error checks are being shared with the companies for training. This is optional in your AI tool settings, and you can opt-out.

There is another danger: If you generate text using AI, and it reproduces copyrighted materials that you then publish, you are infringing on the original copyright holder. That liability is not limited just to the AI company. Republishing carries its own risks. Currently, online sources such as blogs and articles are being crawled by AI and indexing bots, which means they end up in training datasets. Generative AI runs the risk that you will accidentally publish part of another person's blog—even if lightly paraphrased. This is another practical reason to avoid relying on AI-generated text in work you intend to claim as your own in commercial spaces.

### Getting Permission to Use Other People's Content

When you need permission, you'll have to identify the rights holder and ask, ideally in writing. For text, that means contacting the author or the publisher. For lyrics, it means approaching the music publisher or the artist. For images, it means licensing through a stock provider or contacting the photographer or owner. If you can reach the copyright holder and get their attention, some will simply grant you the license generously. Some will require you to pay a licensing fee or a royalty.

When you obtain a license, make sure you get it in writing and that it specifies exactly what you may use, in what formats, in what territories, for how long, and on what terms. And, of course, if you cannot get affirmative permission, then don't use the work. Find something else.

### International Differences in Fair Use

Fair use is a feature of United States law, and it does not exist in the same form everywhere. Many other countries instead recognize a narrower doctrine often called fair dealing, which typically permits unlicensed use only for specific enumerated purposes, such as criticism, review, news reporting, or research. The practical consequence is that a use you might defend as fair in the United States could be infringement under another country's laws. When using the works of a person who is in another country, proceed with more caution.

### Action Steps: Navigating Fair Use and Plagiarism

1. Fair use is a four-factor balancing test applied to specific facts, and any use of another's protected expression carries

## Chapter Eleven

# TRADEMARKS

When I want to be annoying at parties, I correct people's misuse of "copyright" when they really mean "trademark" and vice versa. But while trademarks might include words, images, or symbols, some of which may also be protected by copyrights, they are very different things.

Copyrights protect the content of original creative expression, such as the text inside a book or the image in a photograph, or the notes in a song. A trademark is a way to brand: it is a word, symbol, or image (like a short phrase or an icon) that identifies your brand as the commercial source of whatever it is you sell. Trademarks arise from the use of the mark in commerce and are not protected from mere creation. The purposes of the two also differ: copyright protects a creator from duplication of their work without permission, while trademark protects consumers from confusion about who is behind a product and protects businesses from having their brand identity exploited.

Consider Apple, by way of illustration. The name "Apple" is trademarked by the company, even though it is just a single word—and the trademark is limited to computing, not to all apples. Similarly, Apple's logo of an apple with a bite out of it is trademarked. You cannot use their logo in your designs without permission. But using the word apple doesn't violate copyright because you cannot copyright a single, common word. However, if you copied Apple's code and republished it, you would violate their copyrights (and probably their patents, but I digress).

### What You Can and Can't Trademark

Not everything can be a trademark. To function as a trademark, a term must be distinctive enough to identify a source. Invented words as names make strong trademarks, which is why pharmaceuticals all have crazy nonsense names like Ozempic or Cialis. Arbitrary names are the next strongest marks, like the name Apple for a computer—apples as a fruit aren't normally associated with computers, so the brand becomes distinctive.

Next, you have suggestive names, like Greyhound, which act like metaphors for the service (greyhounds are fast; and a century ago, buses were also considered fast). Suggestive names can usually be trademarked. But merely descriptive names like American Airlines (they are literally an airline in America) can be trademarked only if they acquire brand recognition over time.

Generic terms (the word apple to describe an actual apple) can never be trademarks. As an aside, some trademarks can become generic with enough common use, like the word zipper. Did you know Zipper was the trademarked name for a "slide fastener"? Nobody did; everyone called it a zipper, and that became the generic word for it.

A crucial point for authors is that the title of a single work generally cannot be trademarked. A title is considered descriptive. It takes a lot of popularity—like *Game of Thrones* or *Bridgerton*—to become branded enough to support a trademark. If the title is of a series, that functions better as a trademark because it identifies a line of products that mark a brand.

Logos (the Starbucks mermaid), distinctive imprint names (Netflix), and some slogans (Just Do It) can be trademarked. Your author name, including a pen name, can also be trademarked in the right circumstances. Nora Roberts and J.D. Robb are both trademarked author names for the same writer.

The through-line is that trademark protects identifiers that point to a particular brand as the source of goods. If you really want a trademark for your trophy wall, think first of your series or your indie publishing imprint, rather than individual titles.

### Trade Dress

Trademark protection can extend beyond names, logos, and slogans to trade dress, which is the overall visual appearance of a product or its packaging when that appearance identifies the source. The shape of a Coca-Cola bottle, the distinctive Tiffany blue box, and the look of Apple's retail stores are all protected trade dress. For authors, trade dress is most likely to come up in series branding. A distinctive and consistent visual presentation across a series of covers or web properties, for example, that readers associate with your work at a glance, may function as protectable trade dress. Investing in consistent, distinctive design for a series is good business as well as good marketing.

### Trademark Searching and Registration

Before you commit to a brand, search to make sure it is not

already in use by someone else. Adopting a name that infringes an existing trademark can force a costly rebrand later. A search looks at the national trademark register first. But you should also look at actual marketplace use, since trademark rights can arise from use even without registration (for example, someone could have superior rights to a name simply by having used it first in commerce, even without a federal registration). The United States Patent and Trademark Office's database is free to search for registered marks. Google is a good source for general trade use, as is Amazon for titles and series.

When you search, look for the use of the brand in similar areas of commerce. The same brand can be used in unrelated areas of commerce without violating a trademark. For example, I once owned a law firm that I named Bellatrix, which is the Latin word for warrior, feminized, and also a star in the constellation Orion. Besides my firm, there were other businesses named Bellatrix. But none of them were in legal services, so it was available to use and trademark. And I didn't have to worry about the Harry Potter character Bellatrix Lestrange, except for the number of people who asked me if I named my law firm after her (I did not).

Just like with copyrights, you can hold a common law trademark through use alone, and even enforce it against competitors. When you hold a common law trademark, you can use the TM in a circle symbol to publicly declare it.

Also like copyrights, federal registration confers significant advantages, including a legal presumption of your ownership and exclusive right to use the mark nationwide, public notice of your claim, and stronger enforcement tools. When you register a trademark, you can use the Registered symbol, which is an R in a circle.

You can't use the Registered symbol on an unregistered mark, however.

Registration involves an application that the USPTO examines and decides. The process takes time and is somewhat more expensive than obtaining a copyright. It is highly advisable to use a lawyer who specializes in trademarks to do this. The process is more involved than copyright registration, and the examination process has real pitfalls for the uninitiated. But for an author with a valuable series brand or an established pen name, registering the trademark can be a sound investment. Because, unlike copyright, which has a fixed term, trademark protection can last indefinitely. That means a trademark is a permanent business asset, as long as you keep using it and keep up with the required maintenance filings with the USPTO.

### Trademark Protection Outside the United States

Trademark protection is territorial. A United States trademark registration does not protect your mark in other countries. If you are selling globally, which most authors on Amazon and other international platforms are, your brand may be vulnerable to use or registration by others in foreign markets. Bigger brand authors address this through the Madrid Protocol, an international treaty that allows you to file a single application seeking trademark protection in multiple member countries. It is not cheap, but for authors building a significant international series brand or pen name, it is worth discussing with an appropriately experienced attorney.

### Using Trademarks in Your Creative Work

Authors worry far more than necessary about mentioning real

brands in their works. It's actually unnecessary to create fake brands to avoid trademark liability, and using a fake name won't avoid defamation if that's your concern (see Chapter 7 on this). Generally, you can refer to trademarked brands in your creative work in ordinary, truthful ways without infringing. Because using a brand name to refer to the actual product is the whole point of the brand and its protection—that's a permissible reference. Your characters can drink Coke, drive a Ford, or shop at Home Depot, and that's perfectly acceptable because the use of the trademarks signifies the commercial products and brands they are registered to signify.

As stated a few times in other parts of this book, you can't use a real brand in a way that suggests the brand sponsors, endorses, or is associated with your work. The same thing goes for celebrities. In my novels, for example, my characters listen to Taylor Swift. But Taylor Swift doesn't have a pull quote on my cover (at least not yet—maybe someday).

**Action Steps: Building and Protecting Your Author Brand**

1. Understand the difference between copyright and trademark. Copyright protects your creative expression. Trademark protects the identifiers, names, logos, and slogans, that tell consumers who is behind a product. They serve different purposes and require different strategies.

2. Before you commit to a series name, pen name, or imprint name, search the USPTO trademark database and do a general marketplace search. A conflict you discover before launch is far cheaper to resolve than one you discover

after. Search for use in similar areas of commerce, not just identical names. The same name can coexist in unrelated fields.

3. Think about trademarks in terms of your series and your publishing imprint first, not individual titles. A single title is generally not protectable, but a series name that identifies a line of products can be. Invest in consistent, distinctive design for your series. A recognizable visual identity across a series can function as protectable trade dress.

4. Register your most valuable marks with the USPTO. Federal registration gives you a nationwide presumption of ownership, public notice, and stronger enforcement tools. Use an attorney.

5. Remember that trademark protection can last indefinitely, unlike copyright's fixed term.

6. If you are selling internationally, your U.S. trademark registration does not protect you abroad. Talk to a trademark attorney about the Madrid Protocol if you are building a significant international brand.

7. You don't need to create fake brand names in your fiction to avoid trademark liability. Just don't imply that the brand endorses your work.

Chapter Twelve

# PROTECTING YOUR WORK FROM PIRACY

My debut novel was pirated within two weeks of publishing it. I quickly traced it to an Advanced Review Copy that went out using a well known review service. I had the reader banned from the service, but the damage was already done.

Sooner or later, most authors discover their works on a site offering them for free (or for sale!) without permission. Sometimes you find this out in the worst possible way: you get flagged for plagiarism by Google or terminated for copyright violations by Amazon, which is a nightmare scenario that takes far too long to correct.

When someone steals your work, you will be angry. Worse, you'll be frustrated when you realize that getting your work contained after it has been stolen is a difficult process, and you may not succeed in quashing every illicit copy (in fact, you almost certainly won't). But while pirates happen to everyone, there are some things you can do to protect yourself, get illegal copies and sites taken down, and ensure Amazon doesn't suddenly terminate your account for copyright violations.

### Monitoring Your Works for Piracy

Like other internet scams and thievery, piracy is a fact of the digital age. Most online piracy occurs offshore in countries that do not have the legal structures or financial incentives to control it. Some of the worst offenders use torrent technology and server farms that cannot be reached by interested governments. As a result, unauthorized copies of books, music, movies, courses, and other content circulate widely.

Even though it's offensive to have your work stolen, consider one reality check to ease the sting: People who get your work through pirated sites were never going to pay for it. So, as a practical matter, you've lost nothing. Do the things you need to protect your legitimate sales channels. Then don't worry about pirates—they are just a sign that your marketing is making you visible enough that someone shoplifted your work. Karma will get them someday.

So while I do not recommend driving yourself crazy chasing pirates, still do some monitoring. A light monitoring routine is part of your business maintenance, with an emphasis on light. The first thing you should do is set up a Google Alert for your author names and titles (this will also help you know when you get recommended or blogged about in the wild, which is a fun surprise!).

On a regular schedule (I do it semi-annually), search for your book titles and author name alongside terms like *free, download,* and *PDF* to locate pirate listings. Use incognito browsers with cleared caches so your history doesn't skew results—you'll find more hidden sites that way.

Paid monitoring and takedown services also exist that will scan for infringing copies and send notices on your behalf, which can save time for prolific authors but are fairly expensive. All you need is to find the sites and images that are indexing well enough that you can locate them on search engines. You do not need to conduct exhaustive surveillance of the entire internet, which is neither achievable nor worth the effort.

### The DMCA Takedown Notice Process

Whenever you find someone infringing on your copyright, the very first thing you should do is send a takedown notice, commonly called a DMCA notice. DMCA stands for Digital Millennium Copyright Act. Pirates may ignore the notice, but you will sometimes be surprised. I've had pirates take down my copyrighted work once I called them on it.

But even if you get ignored, it is worth doing because you can use it to leverage delisting on search engines and having hosts and domain registrars shut them down for terms violations. While a pirate may not care, Go Daddy does. I've had many offending sites shut down by registrars and web hosts over the years! (Be aware that well-established pirate sites now run their own servers to handle hosting and domain registration in locales unreachable by law enforcement, so this is not foolproof.)

To be valid, a DMCA takedown notice must contain specific elements: (1) identification of the copyrighted work you own, (2) identification of the infringing material and its location precisely enough for the host to find it (usually a URL), (3) your contact information, (4) a statement that you have a good-faith belief the use is not authorized, (5) a statement made under penalty of perjury that your notice is accurate and that you are the owner or authorized to act for the owner, and (6) your signature. Because the perjury statement is part of the notice, you'll want to ensure you are using a trustworthy template with the correct language.

One thing to be aware of: a recipient of your takedown notice can file a counter-notice disputing your claim. If that happens, the platform or host may restore the content unless you file a lawsuit within a limited window, typically ten to fourteen business days. This doesn't happen often with straightforward piracy, but knowing it exists means you won't be blindsided if it does. I've only had one pirate site try it, but they ultimately took the offending material down after I turned out to be more hassle than the stolen work was worth.

### Reporting to Google and Other Search Engines

After sending your Takedown Notice, head over to Google and search for their deindexing tool. Search engines accept copyright removal and deindexing requests. Once a request is confirmed, Google will deindex the infringing page so that it no longer appears in searches, cutting off much of the traffic that makes piracy profitable. This does not delete the copy from the host, but it makes the copy far harder to find, which addresses much of the practical damage.

### Complain to the Web Host

When a pirate site itself will not cooperate, the company hosting that site often will. Most hosts have to agree to comply with U.S. and E.U. law to do business, and so they have Terms of Service that make piracy a serious terms violation. You can identify the host behind a website through publicly available lookup tools that reveal the hosting provider and related infrastructure, then send your takedown notice to that host's designated abuse or copyright address. After being satisfied that your copyright complaint is well-taken, the host will usually respond by shutting down the offending website and terminating their account.

### Domain Registrar Complaints

Also complain to the domain registrar, which is the company that registered the pirate site's URL or web address. Several times, I've had domains suspended by registrars for clients when I was able to demonstrate copyright infringement, piracy, spoofing, or fraud. Registrars always require proof before freezing a domain, so be prepared to work with them. You can find the registrar for a domain using a Whois lookup.

### Platform-Specific Removal Processes

I've never had a pirate bold enough to pass off my work on a major retailer or distributor. But if they do that to you, you'll need to aggressively flag it directly with the retailer to avoid the duplicate content randomly tripping automated moderation software and killing your account. Retailers and distributors have their own processes for reporting copyright claims, but their rules and contact information for claims are usually easy to find. At worst, it'll be in the website's footer next to their Terms of Service and Privacy Policy.

### Counterfeit Print Copies

Digital piracy gets most of the attention, but counterfeit physical books are a real and growing problem, particularly on Amazon's marketplace, where third-party sellers have passed off counterfeit print copies of popular books to unsuspecting buyers. These copies are usually derived from pirated electronic copies, and the formatting and quality are deeply subpar. You don't want your readers to buy these terrible knock-offs. So be sure to check Amazon (and sometimes eBay) for print copies of your books. If you discover counterfeit print copies of your work, report it to the retailer, send a DMCA notice, and document everything. Amazon has a brand registry and a counterfeit reporting mechanism that you can use.

### When to Hire a Lawyer

I have been hired to handle these steps by clients for at least fifteen years. They typically want to use me because my legal letterhead is taken more seriously. If your Takedown Notice is ignored, and hosts and registrars and platforms are also ignoring you, the magic letterhead is sometimes worth hiring a lawyer for.

The other times when you might want to use a lawyer is when the theft is creating catastrophic consequences for you or your business, such as getting you locked out of accounts and platforms that are the lifeblood of your income. Another time is when it indicates significant identity theft or spoofing. Because identity theft and spoofing can leave you with significant liabilities. For example, I once found a scam website using my picture, name, and professional background to sell a fake financial service—and if I let that stand unanswered, I would've had to fear prosecution, civil liability, or complaints against my law license.

### Preventative Measures

A few preventative measures can reduce piracy. The main one is to use technical protections such as digital rights management or visible watermarks. Amazon's digital rights management software encrypts your books so that they can only be read on Kindle apps or devices with the purchase key. The books cannot be printed, shared, or downloaded to other services. This is only controversial inasmuch as it keeps the buyer of the book locked into using Kindle technology (although the apps are free) to read a book they'd purchased.

If you are selling directly, watermarking can at least help trace the source of a leak. It also educates and shames buyers who purchase through piracy sites. If you distribute through Bookfunnel, you can choose how the watermarking presents. A visible watermark on the title page is a non-disruptive way to ensure subsequent readers know they've stolen the work, and from whom—because the watermark lists the name and address of the buyer who downloaded your book to begin with. If you distribute through Adobe, you can put even more robust security measures in place, including passwords that stay with the document and prevents subsequent buyers from opening it.

### Action Steps: Protecting Your Work from Piracy

1. Set up Google Alerts for your author name, pen names, and book titles now, before you need them. Alerts catch piracy, but they also catch good news like recommenda-

tions and reviews.

2. Do a semi-annual piracy search using your book titles and author name alongside terms like free, download, and PDF. Use an incognito browser with a cleared cache to get unfiltered results.

3. When you find infringing content, send a DMCA takedown notice immediately. Use a trustworthy template that includes all required elements, and pay attention to the perjury statement, which must be accurate.

4. After sending your takedown notice, submit a deindexing request to Google and other search engines.

5. If the pirate ignores you, escalate to the web host and the domain registrar. Most hosts and registrars take copyright complaints seriously because piracy violates their Terms of Service. Use a Whois lookup to identify them.

6. Watch for counterfeit print copies, not just digital piracy. If you find them on Amazon or elsewhere, report them through the platform's counterfeit reporting mechanism.

7. Enable digital rights management on your Kindle titles. It is not a perfect solution, but it raises the barrier to casual piracy significantly.

8. If you sell direct, use watermarking through Bookfunnel or Adobe to trace the source of leaks and deter casual redistribution.

9. If your takedown efforts are being ignored across the board, or if piracy is threatening your accounts or income, hire a lawyer. Legal letterhead gets attention that author emails do not.

10. Keep piracy in perspective. People who download pirated books were never going to buy them. Protect your legitimate sales channels, take reasonable steps to address infringement, and don't let pirates consume your time and energy beyond that.

Chapter Thirteen

# PUBLISHING RIGHTS, WHOLESALERS, AND CONSIGNMENT

When I was first in law school, my professors kept telling us that property rights are "bundles." I didn't quite understand that until I looked at a piece of string cheese. I'll explain: When you write something, you own the copyright—that's the stick of string cheese. But you have the option of peeling off bits of cheese and eating them individually, or you can sell those pieces, or give them away, or spread them on different plates.

Perhaps you didn't realize it, but every single author selling their work is peeling off strings of cheese from their original mozzarella stick of copyright. So while I'll spare you any more cheesy metaphors, the rest of this chapter will be a quick primer on the types of rights you're sectioning off and selling as a normal part of your business.

### First Publication Rights

First publication rights are exactly what they sound like: the right to publish your work first. This is common in the periodical and short-fiction markets, where a magazine may purchase the right to publish your piece first, but allow you to republish it later, either immediately, after some time has passed, or as part of a larger work.

> >>> Traditional publishers will sometimes purchase the copyright, and not just a license. There may be carve-outs for territories, translations, and adaptations. Under no circumstances should you negotiate a traditional publishing agreement on your own—and usually you can't, anyway, because agents are required to approach publishers.

If you are offered a hybrid or small publisher contract, it is not normal for them to claim the entire copyright, as opposed to a bounded license. Such terms mean either that they are unsophisticated or that they are taking advantage of authors. Again, a lawyer is recommended.

### Exclusivity

Exclusivity means you agree to publish or distribute your work with a specific partner only and at the exclusion of all others. You're marrying that publisher, and it's monogamous. Exclusivity is usually time-limited, although publishing contracts can be perpetual. It is also usually bounded by territory, language, and format (e.g. foreign sales, translations, movie, and audiobook rights might not be included). A common example: Kindle Select is an exclusive distribution agreement with Kindle for ebooks for ninety days at a time.

### Duration and Reversion

Many licensing agreements are perpetual (e.g. the license you get on stock photos), but most have a defined duration and a way to get the rights back. A reversion clause specifies when and how your rights return to you. Sometimes it is after a set period of time. But it can also occur when sales fall below a threshold, when the work goes out of print, the publisher bankrupts or dissolves, or some other legal or situational trigger.

### Subsidiary Rights

Subsidiary rights are the secondary rights beyond the primary edition, including things like audio, foreign translation, film and television adaptations, serialization, and merchandizing, and they can be more valuable than the primary book rights themselves. Publishers often seek to acquire these subsidiary rights, which is why you should use a lawyer or an agent when negotiating these deals.

### Territory and Language Rights

Rights can be divided geographically and linguistically. That means an author might use different publishers and distributors to sell their work in certain countries or to sell translations without disturbing other contracts. For example, the Spanish version of your book sold in Mexico may be on a distinct agreement to your same book being sold in English in the United Kingdom, with neither contract causing conflict with the other.

### Film and Television Adaptation Rights

Film, television, and other adaptation rights are the right to turn your work into other media. While a lucrative adaptation is rare, they are extraordinarily valuable when they happen. Because of that potential, adaptation rights deserve particular care, and you should be reluctant to grant them away cheaply as part of a broad agreement.

### Audiobook Production and Narration Rights

Audiobooks are a rapidly expanding format, and the agreements surrounding their production involve distinct rights because multiple creators are involved. An audiobook production agreement governs how the audio edition gets made and who holds the resulting rights because, in addition to the author's copyrights, the performer who records the narration has copyrights to the recording, and the sound engineers who mix the final production and add other creative elements also have copyrights.

Audiobook production agreements typically come in two main flavors: a work-for-hire arrangement (where you pay for the actors and producers and keep all the rights) and a royalty-share arrangement (where you partner with the actors and producers and split the proceeds).

Platform-based production exchanges formalize these arrangements through their own agreements, which can include exclusivity commitments and multi-year terms that determine where your audiobook may be sold and for how long. Professional audiobook production contracts, where you hire a studio or producer directly, should clearly assign you the rights to the finished product and define the deliverables and payment. Beyond that, certain distributors will require exclusivity and royalty shares (e.g. Audible), often with multi-year terms.

### Distribution Agreements

Distribution agreements determine how your books reach the market through wholesalers, distributors, other channels besides the direct sale platforms and hosts that you control. Common direct sale platforms and hosts include your own website or blog, Substack, Shopify, and Payhip.

Common wholesalers include IngramSpark, Draft2Digital print, and the traditional Big 5 publishers. Common retail distributors include Amazon, Google Play, Apple Books, Barnes & Noble, Wal-Mart and Hudson News. Other than the indie publishing you do with Amazon, Google Play, and Draft2Digital, distribution agreements should be reviewed and negotiated by agents or lawyers.

### Wholesalers vs. Retailers: Understanding the Difference

When it comes to print distribution, you need to understand the distinction between wholesalers and retailers. A retailer sells directly to the end reader (they're the bookstore). A wholesaler sits in the middle, buying or listing books, handling printing and fulfillment of large orders, and supplying them to retailers. IngramSpark is the wholesaler of choice for most bookstores and libraries. Wholesalers will set a substantial discount off suggested sales price—which is set by the retailer—because that discount is what funds the retailer's margin and the wholesaler's cut. If you've ever seen a product that lists "Manufacturer's Suggested Retail Price" or MSRP, what you are seeing is the wholesale price plus a markup.

For example, if you sell a print book for an MSRP of $20, a wholesaler will require you to license it to the wholesaler at 55% off, or for a $9 gross royalty. From that $9, they will deduct manufacturing (printing, shipping, handling) costs and lost sales caused by returns. What remains is your profit. The $11 difference between the $9 wholesale price and the $20 retail price is the profit that the retailer gets after the wholesaler's cut. When you add in $6 for printing, shipping, and handling, your share of the sale of a $20 book is $3. This model mostly makes sense if you are moving a high volume of books through big-box retailers. Small retailers are nice to have, but won't pay much if you're going through a wholesaler.

### Local Bookstore Consignment

A more typical way to sell through small retailers is via consignment at your local independent bookshop. Consignment is an arrangement where you provide an agreed number of copies to the store but retain ownership of the books until they sell. The store takes a cut of any books of yours they sell. When the consignment period ends, The bookshop returns any remaining inventory to you.

A consignment agreement should spell out the split, the consignment period, who bears the risk of damaged or lost inventory, how unsold copies are returned, and how and when you are paid and given a sales report. For more information on negotiating and entering a consignment agreement with local small businesses, download the companion *Beyond the Basics* resources guide.

### Syndicating Across Platforms

If your work isn't subject to an exclusivity agreement, you can syndicate it. Syndication means distributing your work across multiple platforms and channels. A common example are Substack authors who syndicate their articles to Medium, or vice versa.

Distributing the same work across several online platforms creates a technical issue worth understanding: duplicate content and the risk of being flagged for plagiarism by a bot. When identical book descriptions and pages appear on many sites, search engines must decide which version to favor.

When the platforms are trusted by Google (like Substack and Medium), syndication of duplicate content rarely produces a formal penalty; so by all means, do it. But help Google out by identifying which work is canon whenever technically possible. This isn't a book about SEO, but a bit of searching online will yield instructions on how to designate a canonical link.

### Keeping Track

So you've got a bunch of agreements distributing your works widely. First of all, well done! Now, do yourself a favor and come up with a tracking system. You need to know what rights each agreement grants and when the agreements are up for termination or renewal. A spreadsheet will do. The resource guide links you to a sample. Check your tracker regularly and maintain your agreements as they come up for termination and renewal. Or have your assistant do it, moneybags.

**Action Steps: Managing Your Rights and Distribution**

1. Understand your rights bundle. Your copyright is divisible by format, territory, language, duration, first prints, and exclusivity.

2. Never sign a traditional publishing agreement or major distribution agreement without a lawyer reviewing it.

3. Guard your subsidiary rights. Audio, foreign translation, film, and adaptation rights can be more valuable than your primary edition.

4. Know your exclusivity commitments before you syndicate. But otherwise, you have the right to distribute your work wherever you choose, however you choose.

5. Audiobook agreements can be works-for-hire or royalty-share agreements.

6. Understand the economics of the wholesale trade before you enter it. Wide distribution into bookstores and libraries means deeper discounts and the risk of returns.

7. If you sell through local bookstores, use a written consignment agreement.

8. Maintain a contracts tracking system and stay on top of renewals, expirations, and overlap.

# BEYOND THE BASICS

## A Free Resource Companion

Throughout this book, I have pointed you toward a companion resource guide for the deeper dives, sample documents, and practical tools that would have bogged down the main text.

*Beyond the Basics* is free to download as a PDF, using the below QR code or by following the link. This link will bring you directly to my Payhip shop, and you can complete the purchase and download for no charge. While Payhip will require your customer information, this is not a newsletter opt-in. Email will stay limited to information about this purchase and the option for downloading future updates.

LINK—> https://link.acidsquirrelmedia.com/beyondbasics

**What's Inside**

The guide is organized to follow the same path as this book, so you can jump to whatever you need. Here is what you will find.

1. FAQs About Amazon's Terms and Kindle Select Exclusivity. A plain-English walkthrough of the key parts of Amazon's terms of service, including how KDP Select exclusivity actually works, and how to handle an unexpected account termination.

2. Recommended Software Stack for Compliance and Ease. The tools I actually use for my author business.

3. Operating Agreements and Contracts FAQ. How to find reliable templates that conform with your local laws without borrowing from unvetted sources like random websites on Google, your friend's small business, or AI chatbots.

4. Business Formation and Payroll Setup Checklist.

5. Multi-Author Agreements and Partnership FAQs. A closer look at what changes when you write with partners, including the differences between partnerships, multi-member LLCs, and joint ventures, and the questions to settle in writing before you publish a co-authored work.

6. A Deeper Dive on U.S. Sales Taxes. The longer treatment of sales tax nexus, marketplace facilitator rules, and the

Merchant of Record question that I pulled out of Chapter 3 so it would not swallow the chapter. For authors who sell direct and want to understand the machinery.

7. A Deeper Dive on Disclaimers. Where to find sample disclaimer language and guidance on when you need one. Not a substitute for professional advice, but a strong starting point.

8. A Deeper Dive on Terms of Service, Refund Policies, and Privacy Policies. Where to find reputable templates for the core legal documents your website needs.

9. Website Accessibility Checkers. A curated list of the free and paid tools I recommend for testing your site against accessibility standards, plus how to spot website developers who over-engineer fixes or provide tools that don't do the job.

10. Consignment Agreements FAQs. The practical questions to raise with an independent bookstore before you place your books on consignment, including splits, consignment periods, risk of loss, returns, and getting paid, and where to get contracts.

11. Contracts Tracker Template. What it should include, what software to use when you don't like spreadsheets, and where to find templates.

12. Dispute Resolution FAQ: From Demand Letters to Small Claims. What to do when a disagreement starts tilting

toward litigation, how to make your first moves wisely, and links to low-cost resolution resources.

### Bonus Coupons

***The Author's Legal Form Pack***. For authors who would rather start from a solid draft than a blank page, I offer a pack of core business and publishing agreements, demand letters, and contract clauses specifically curated for author businesses and drafted in plain language. Readers of this book get a coupon for $50 off *The Author's Legal Form Pack* (full retail price is $347, which is less than half my hourly rate as a lawyer). The coupon code and purchase link are inside the resource guide.

***Help! I've Been Sued! Ten Steps to Avoid Disaster.*** The resource guide comes with a 10% coupon off my book dedicated to helping those who find themselves in litigation and need immediate guidance.

### A Living Document

The law does not hold still, and neither do internet platforms, taxes, or scammers. A book is fixed at the moment it goes to press (or is downloaded), but the resource guide is something I can update more frequently. I update it at least annually, along with the *Author's Legal Form Pack*, and you can download it more than once. If you do not want to receive notices of updates, you can opt-out at any time.

Thank you for reading, and for taking your business as seriously as the craft of writing itself. Your work matters. Don't let the AI grind you down.

# About the Author

Alicia I. Dearn, Esq. works as a trial lawyer, entrepreneur, and author. She publishes on topics of law, business, politics, and memoir. "Amelia Elliot" is the pen name for Ms. Dearn's fictional works in women's and literary fiction, romance, sci-fi, and political and legal thrillers. She lives with her husband, three big dogs, and three riotous kittens.

AliciaDearn.com

NoAIJustExperience.com

***Did this book help you? Leave a review!***

Please support independent authors and small publishers by leaving ratings and reviews with the retailers of purchase. It's one of the best ways to thank and support independent creatives. **Your positive feedback means the world to me.**

www.ingramcontent.com/pod-product-compliance
Lightning Source LLC
Chambersburg PA
CBHW071341230926
51846CB00002B/415
* 9 7 8 1 9 6 5 2 8 2 0 8 3 *